What to Do

IF A BIRD FLIES IN THE HOUSE

What to Do

IF A BIRD FLIES IN THE HOUSE

AND **72** OTHER THINGS YOU OUGHT TO KNOW BY NOW

ELIZABETH NIX
and
ELIZABETH HURCHALLA

 ST. MARTIN'S GRIFFIN 🦅 NEW YORK

www.stmartins.com

Book design by Jonathan Bennett

Illustrations by Wendy Letven

Library of Congress Cataloging-in-Publication Data

Nix, Elizabeth.
    What to do if a bird flies in the house and 72 other things you ought to know by now / Elizabeth Nix and Elizabeth Hurchalla.—1st ed.
       p. cm.
    ISBN 0-312-30939-2
    1. Women—Life skills guides. I. Hurchalla, Elizabeth. II. Title.

HQ1221 .N57 2003
646.7'0082—dc21

2002036896

First Edition: April 2003

10   9   8   7   6   5   4   3   2   1

CONTENTS

- -

INTRODUCTION

- -

What to Do If a Bird Flies in the House and 72 Other Things You Ought to Know By Now will clue you in on how to do all the stuff you always thought you'd have learned by the time you became an adult, but never actually did. Concentrating on real-life daily dilemmas, *What to Do If a Bird Flies in the House* gives you advice you'll actually use, on everything from buying a diamond to house-training a puppy. Don't want to become an auto mechanic, but want to know enough not to get ripped off by one? Don't want a botany degree, but want to know how not to kill a houseplant? Don't want a cookbook featuring eighteen ways to prepare lobster, but want to know how to eat it if it shows up on a menu? This book is for you.

With this book, you'll gain just enough knowledge to march into any situation with confidence and grace. *What to Do If a Bird Flies in the House* is finishing school for the twenty-first century: it'll teach you a little charm, sure, but it'll also teach you about cars, home repair, and everything else you need to know to be a polished, independent woman today. Although many of the topics we cover could fill books of their own (and do), we realize you don't have a bunch of free Saturdays to sit around studying manuals on how to buy a used car or burglar-proof your house. So we've done all the work for you, consulting experts and distilling volumes of information down to just what you need to know. Inside, you'll find the easiest, most straightforward way to approach each situation, featuring step-by-step instructions and diagrams to make it as simple as possible to become an instant authority.

We understand your desire to do it all—or at least to *know* how to do it all. Although we're both professionally successful, when it comes to fixing a flat or knowing whether to sip cabernet or chardonnay with our tuna tartare, we've found ourselves coming up short more often than we'd like to admit. If you ask us, true confidence comes from knowledge, and the first step to living a better, fuller life is just learning how. That's the inspiration behind *What to Do If a Bird Flies in the House*—to fill you in on everything you might have missed along the way.

HOW TO GET A STUCK RING OFF

Rings on your fingers, bells on your toes. . . . Although bells on your toes may cause you more problems in the long run (you're a real killjoy at surprise parties, aren't you?), that ring on your finger can be tricky too. Oh, it's swell when it's on—it's just when you try to take it off that things can get sticky. Here's how to get a ring unstuck:

1. Don't try to force the ring off, since this may just make your finger swell more. Instead, raise your hand to eye level. Then wrap some ice in a washcloth or a couple of paper towels and hold it around the finger the ring's on. This should reduce the swelling and help you get the thing off.

2. If the ring still won't budge, run your hands under cold water, soap them up, and rub above and below the ring. Then twist the ring like you're unscrewing it instead of just pulling it straight off.

WHAT TO DO IF YOU SEE A BEAR
IN THE WOODS

2 –

The bad news about bears is that they can run faster than you can. The good news is that they're solitary creatures who would much rather spend the day foraging for nuts and berries than bumping into you amidst the birches. Fortunately, you need never meet in the first place, provided you take a few precautions when hiking in bear country: travel in groups of at least three people; clap, talk, sing loudly, or hang a bell from your pack to avoid surprising bears; make sure any food and other scented stuff (like deodorant, toothpaste, and trash) is stored in Ziploc bags inside your pack; and hightail it the other way if you see any fresh tracks, droppings, or animal carcasses lying around. If, despite your best efforts, you still run into a bear, here's what to do:

1. Remain calm. Most bears don't want to attack you; they just want to make sure you're not a threat. Even if a bear charges at you, stand your ground and try not to panic: chances are, the bear is bluffing and will turn away at the last second.

2. Don't run! Running can result in an attack—instead, back away slowly. If it's impossible to back away or if your actions appear to be pissing off the bear, wait until it moves away. Always leave the bear an escape route.

3. Avoid eye contact, sudden movements, yelling, and anything else that the bear might interpret as a sign of aggression. If the bear thinks you're challenging it, it might try to fight.

4. If the bear does attack—don't worry, this is very rare—defend yourself aggressively with your hands, a stick, a rock, or anything else lying around that you think might help. Do whatever it takes to let the bear know you aren't easy prey and make it give up. (If you've heard that you're supposed to lie down and play dead, you're right—but only if you're dealing with grizzly bears, which are much less common than the black bear found all over the United States. Grizzlies tend to be larger and more powerful; however, they're also quite rare and found in only a few northwestern states.)

5. Once the bear backs down and starts to leave the area, stay where you are until it's gone; if the bear sees you move, it might attack again.

HOW TO GET TICKETS
TO A SOLD—OUT CONCERT

3 ─

So your all-time favorite band/opera singer/mime troupe is coming to town and you absolutely have to be there. Trouble is, the tickets sold out in ten minutes—and you didn't get one. But "sold out" doesn't necessarily mean *all* tickets are taken. Here's how to improve your chances of seeing the show (without succumbing to scalpers):

1. Check with the box office or ticket seller every day for at least a week or two after the tickets are "sold out." Most likely, some credit cards won't get approved and some orders will be canceled, so those tickets will go back on sale.

2. On the day of the performance, call or visit the box office a few hours before showtime, when many venues release extra tickets held for their own staff, the artist's guest list, and/or ticketing mix-ups. It's a long shot, but you could get lucky and score a seat.

3. Another option, although pretty pricey, is to try a ticket-broker service. These services acquire tickets for a variety of popular entertainment and sports events and then resell them for a premium. You can locate brokers by typing "ticket brokers" into any online search engine or by looking for ads in the arts or lifestyle section of your newspaper. Not all services are legit, however; check with the National Association of Ticket Brokers (www.natb.org) to find a trustworthy company in your area.

WHAT TO DO IF YOU SPILL A DRINK
ON YOUR COMPUTER KEYBOARD

 -

Friends don't let friends drink and use hard drives. Hey, spills can kill your keyboard, so if you do knock a beverage onto it, don't waste time crying over spilled milk (or mochaccino, as the case may be). Instead, take steps to minimize the damage:

1. If the spill is on your desktop keyboard, make sure your hands are dry, then unplug the keyboard from the computer.

2. Dab the affected keys with a slightly damp cloth, being careful not to get any moisture underneath them.

3. Flip the keyboard upside down to drain and let it dry completely for at least twenty-four hours. If you can't function without your keyboard for that long, you can dry it off with a hair dryer, but use a cool setting—you don't want any of the keys to get hot.

4. Reconnect the keyboard to the computer and see if it works. If not, and it's water you spilled, look,

you've done all you could; at least keyboards are relatively inexpensive to replace.

5. If it's coffee, soda, or another sticky drink, on the other hand, remove the keys that got spilled on. On most keyboards, you can pop off a key by wedging a screwdriver under it and pulling up. But first, make sure you know where to put the keys back—draw a diagram if you have to. And don't even try taking off the space bar, enter key, shift keys, or any other large keys, since they can be very tough to put back into place. Clean the detached keys with Q-tips dampened with water, then carefully swab the surface of the keyboard under the keys you've removed to get rid of any sticky residue. Allow the keys to dry completely before putting them back on, then reconnect the computer to the keyboard and hope it works this time.

6. If you spill something on your laptop keyboard, you are one unlucky lady, because liquid on a laptop can make its way into critical internal parts like the motherboard or hard drive and cause serious damage. Don't try to take the laptop apart and clean up the mess yourself. Instead, make sure your hands are dry, then turn off the computer, unplug it, remove the battery, and contact the manufacturer or a service representative for help.

HOW TO FIND THE NORTH STAR

5 --

Twinkle, twinkle, little star, how I wonder where you are. For all the fame the North Star claims, few actually know how to find it. Most stars rise and set, just like the sun and moon. But the North Star, also known as Polaris, is like the hub of a wheel—it stays put in the northern sky while other stars circle around it. That's why if you're facing Polaris, you know you're facing north. And in the U.S., as long as the sky is clear, you should be able to see the North Star any time of the night, any night of the year. So, if you get lost and you've left home without your compass—again—here's how to find your guiding star:

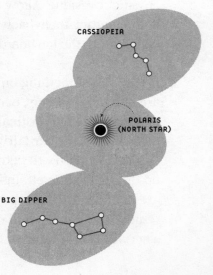

1. Locate the seven stars that form the Big Dipper—look for the rectangular bowl and angled handle.

2. Draw a line from the bottom star on the outside of the bowl to the top star on the outside, then extend that line about five times its length up from the bowl, and you'll be very near the North Star. (If you look at the sky a few hours later, the Big Dipper will appear to have rotated to a new position, but the two stars on the outside of the bowl will still point to Polaris.)

3. To double-check that you've got the right star, find the constellation Cassiopeia, a group of five bright stars shaped like a lopsided "M" (or "W" when it's low in the sky). Cassiopeia revolves slowly around Polaris and is always almost directly opposite the Big Dipper. The North Star is straight out from Cassiopeia's center star, about the same distance as from the Big Dipper.

HOW TO AVOID
GETTING A SPEEDING TICKET

 6 –

Want a surefire guarantee you'll never get another speeding ticket for the rest of your driving days? Don't speed. Look, speeding can lead to accidents—not to mention, uh, speeding tickets. But if you do it anyway and get busted, there *are* ways to sweet-talk the cops who stop you and decrease your chances of getting slapped with a serious fine:

1. If you're speeding and you suddenly notice a police car in your rearview mirror, gradually slow down and give the officer a little wave so he knows you see him, as though you'd like to thank him for helping you realize you were going a little too fast. Sometimes just that small gesture of acknowledgment and respect will be enough to get the police to move on.

2. If the cop stays right behind you and still seems to want you to pull over, do so before he turns the sirens on—if it's a big production just to get you to stop, he's already going to be pissed. Carefully drive

onto the right shoulder and get over as far as you can. Remember, the cop has to approach the driver's side window. Making it dangerous to do so will not help your cause.

3. If you're wearing sunglasses, take them off. How are you going to convince the cop to give you a break if you can't even go to the effort of making eye contact?

4. If it's nighttime, turn on the interior light in the car so the officer doesn't have to wonder whether there's a gun on the passenger seat.

5. Turn off the radio.

6. Roll down your window all the way.

7. Put your hands on the steering wheel at ten and two o'clock. Although the cop is going to need your license and registration, don't reach for them until asked. Again, if your hands are in sight, you're obviously not reaching for a weapon, hiding drugs, or doing anything else a respectable citizen who should be let go wouldn't do.

8. If there are passengers in the car, tell them to put their hands on their laps and let you do the talking.

9. When the cop comes to your window, say, "Good afternoon [or morning or evening, obviously], Officer." A friendly greeting may put the cop in a more lenient state of mind.

10. If the cop asks if you know how fast you were going, say some variation of, "I'm not sure, Officer, but I know I must have been speeding or you wouldn't have stopped me. I guess I wasn't paying as much attention as I should have been, but it wasn't intentional, and it won't happen again." Then shut up. If the officer launches into a lecture, sit there and nod your head. Most people who are pulled over pretend they have no idea why. This does nothing but annoy the officer, who knows damn well that you know damn well that you were doing your best Mario Andretti impersonation mere moments before. Instead, disarm the cop by showing respect, admitting that you screwed up, and promising to cut it out.

11. If you're feeling particularly nervy, you could even try this: "Officer, I know I was going faster than I should have been, but could you please follow me to the nearest rest area and give me the ticket there? I'm sorry, but I really, really have to go!" Then ask for directions to the closest place with a

restroom. Chances are good that the officer will just give you a warning rather than waste time following you around. If you are let go, however, *do* in fact stop at the next rest area, just in case the cop's keeping an eye on you.

12. If the cop simply asks to see your license and registration (which you should always have easily accessible) before turning to head back to the patrol car, make sure you plead your case while you still can. Because each one has its own serial number, a ticket that's already written can't be ripped up, so it's imperative that you do whatever convincing you're going to do before the officer goes to fill out your ticket.

HOW TO CHANGE YOUR NAME

 –

A rose is a rose by any other name, but Rose by another name might be Anastasia. It's easy to change your name if you're getting married or divorced, since it can be an automatic part of the process, but switching your name for other reasons—because you want to take on a name that's easier to pronounce, go by a stage name, change your identity to escape an abusive relationship, or just be called something other than the birth name you've always hated—requires more work. Here's what to do:

1. Choose a new name that's legit. You can't pick a name that would interfere with someone else's rights or be intentionally confusing, meaning you can't legally call yourself Angelina Jolie or a punctuation mark, number, or symbol (Prince's little stunt notwithstanding). Don't get any funny ideas about making a name change for fraudulent purposes like to avoid paying debts, keep from being sued, or get away with a crime.

2. Contact the clerk's office of your local court (look in the blue government pages of your phone book) to find out if you have to get a court order to legally change your name. In some states you don't have to do anything except change your name by usage, which means you just start using a new name in all aspects of your life. However, getting a new passport or other types of identification documents can be tough or impossible if you change your name by usage only, so even if that's an option in your state, getting a court order is probably worth the effort.

3. If you are required (or decide) to get a court order, fill out the necessary forms and make copies of them for your records before turning them in to the court clerk. You'll also need to file a request for a hearing in front of a judge (which should take place about six weeks later) and probably pay a small filing fee.

4. Follow the court's rules for giving public notice of your name change by placing an announcement in a newspaper in the county where you live; you'll have to show proof of publication at your hearing. Generally, your announcement has to run for at

least three consecutive weeks. However, if you're a victim of domestic violence or child abuse and don't want to be found, you're exempt from this requirement altogether.

5. Go to your court hearing. The judge will review your petition and most likely sign a decree granting your name change.

6. Notify everyone you deal with of your new moniker and get your records updated (whether you've changed your name by usage or by court order). In some situations, it will only take a phone call; in other cases, a copy of your court order may be required. Get a driver's license first and then a new Social Security card. Once you've got these, it'll be easier to change your other records. Here's who else needs to know about your new name:

- Bureau of records or vital statistics in the state where you were born (to change your birth certificate: do a Web search for "Department of Health" preceded by the name of the state for more information)
- Department of Motor Vehicles (to change your car registration)
- Post office

- Employer
- Credit card companies and any other companies that send you bills
- Bank and other financial institutions
- Any company or individual you have a contract with
- Doctors
- Lawyer
- Insurance agency
- Registrar of Voters (do a Web search for "Registrar of Voters" preceded by the name of the county and state you live in for more information)
- Alma mater
- Internal Revenue Service
- U.S. State Department (to change your passport: go to state.gov for more information)

7. Hang on to your old identification documents—in case you need them to prove who you used to be.

HOW TO TWEEZE YOUR EYEBROWS

8 – – – – – – – – – – – – – – – – – – –

Never underestimate the power of a woman, a kind word, or a well-groomed eyebrow. Okay, so brows don't attract as much attention as, say, the eyes or mouth ("Your eyes are like limpid pools; your lips, like rubies; your brows . . . um, well, they're really nice"), but a proper pluck can do much to make your peepers pop and polish your look. Ignore your brows no longer! Here's how to tweeze them right:

1. Take a shower or press a hot washcloth to your brow for a few minutes pre-pluck to ward off the irritation of tweezing. Don't numb the area with ice, though, or the pores will close and just make tweezing tougher.

2. Position a pencil next to your nostril and hold it straight up to the brow—that's where your eyebrow should begin. Repeat on the other side. Using that as a guide, pluck any stray hairs between brows. Always tweeze in the direction hair grows.

3. Angle the pencil diagonally from your nostril to just past the outside corner of your eye—that's where the brow should end. Pluck any stray hairs beyond that point.

4. Position the pencil next to your nostril and hold it so it extends to the outside edge of your iris when you're looking straight ahead—that's where the highest part of the brow's arch should be. Using that and your brows' natural curve as your guide, tweeze under brows. To avoid tweezing one brow more than the other, pluck a few hairs at a time from each side. Just don't make brows too thin or try to drastically change their natural shape—it'll look unnatural, for starters, but not only that, plucked hairs don't always grow back.

5. If you have long brow hairs, brush them straight up with an eyebrow comb or toothbrush and trim them with nail scissors.

6. Maintain brow shape with tweezing touch-ups every other day.

HOW TO OPEN A BOTTLE OF CHAMPAGNE

9

The diva in you knows it's just a matter of time before you're called on to christen a ship with champers as the crowd cheers and a band plays on. Meanwhile, assuming you actually want to *drink* your champagne rather than just smash it on random boat hulls for practice, it's probably best to stick with a more conventional (and less violent) method of opening bottles of bubbly. Here's how:

1. Get out your champagne glasses and a cloth napkin or dish towel.

2. Pull off the foil around the cork.

3. Pointing the top of the bottle away from yourself (and any bystanders), carefully untwist and take off the wire muzzle that holds the cork in place.

4. Keep your thumb firmly on the cork, which could shoot off unexpectedly, and twist the *bottle* to ease

the cork out. It should come off with a whisper or sigh, not a loud pop.

5. As soon as the cork is off, quickly cover the top of the bottle with your napkin and have a glass at the ready, just in case the bottle overflows.

Can't even keep a cactus from keeling over? Fear not: just as with any healthy relationship, the trick is to pay attention to your plant's basic needs (water, food, light, warmth, and humidity), but not smother it with too much of a good thing. Here's how to keep your houseplants their happiest:

1. Let there be light—as long as it's the right amount. Check your plant's care instructions, consult a plant book, or look on the Web to find out if it prefers lots of sun, medium sun, or shade. The brightest spot in any home is usually near a window facing south, so position your plant accordingly. Remember that light intensity varies with the seasons, so a plant located in an east window during the summer may require southern exposure in winter. Also keep in mind that light usually strikes the plant from only one side, so turn it periodically to keep it growing upright instead of bending toward the sun.

2. Keep your home at the temperature plants prefer: between sixty and seventy degrees Fahrenheit during the day and five to ten degrees cooler at night. Plants don't like sudden changes in temperature or hot or cold air drafts, so keep them away from radiators as well as window ledges where they'd be exposed to frosty conditions in winter.

3. If you see your plant's leaves curling and drying up, better increase the humidity in the air: use a room humidifier, mist-spray leaves early in the day (leaf disease can develop if leaves remain wet overnight), stand plants on a tray of moist pebbles, or move plants to a high-humidity area such as a bathroom or kitchen.

4. To prevent overwatering, give your plant a thorough drink only when its potting mixture starts to dry out, and don't water it again until it's dried out again, since watering frequently in small doses isn't good for plants. Neglecting to water your plants is bad, but giving them too much to drink can be even worse and lead to root rot.

5. Fertilize your plants regularly. A good meal of Miracle-Gro or another plant food every two to

three weeks suits most plants, but always check
feeding guidelines for your specific plant, since too
much fertilizer can damage it. And only feed it
during active growth periods, which usually means
spring through fall (though plants that bloom in
winter should be fed during their flowering period).

6. Repot the plant when it gets too big for its current
container. Most houseplants come in small plastic
containers, which they'll quickly outgrow. If the
roots are poking through the hole in the bottom of
the container or over the surface of the soil, it's time
to move up to the next size pot. However, don't put
the plant in the largest one you can find, thinking
it'll grow into it—the excess soil will just become
waterlogged and stale. And never use dirt from your
garden to repot the plant, since it can contain bugs,
weeds, and disease; use fresh commercial potting
mixture instead.

7. When you get a new plant, carefully inspect its
leaves, stems, and soil for creepy-crawly pests. And
whenever you've put a plant outside to soak up the
summer sun for a while, look it over closely for
insects before bringing it back inside. If you find a
few leaves or stems have been infested, remove and
discard them. If you spot insects in the soil, get rid

of them by repotting. If you see more than a few
bugs on the leaves, try spraying them off with water.
If that doesn't take care of it, follow up with an
insecticidal soap (available at garden supply stores)
or a homemade soap spray made from a teaspoon of
dishwashing liquid and two cups of water. If all else
fails, you may want to try a pesticide spray.

8. Every few weeks, clean off your plant's leaves to get
   rid of dust. Use a soft, damp cloth on plants with
   smooth leaves, and a small, dry paintbrush on fuzzy-
   leaved plants such as African violets (getting the
   fuzz wet could harm the leaves). At the same time,
   remove any damaged leaves and faded flowers.

Words may be coming out of his mouth, but it's often the rest of him that tells the real story. So if you want to know what a guy really thinks of you, don't ask him—watch him. Here, the basics to decode his body's subtle signals:

1. Look at how his body is positioned in relation to yours. Is he standing or sitting the same way you are? Is he leaning forward? If so, he's interested in you. Are his legs, arms, or feet crossed? Is he leaning back? His interest is elsewhere.

2. Watch his head. If it's tilted down, he disagrees with what you have to say. If it's tilted back, he thinks he's too good for you. But if it's tilted to the side? He thinks you're the ant's pants.

3. Follow his feet. Are they pointed toward you? If he's standing, is the foot nearest you the one he's putting his weight on? Hey, he's into you. However, if his feet are pointed in another direction or he's standing

with his weight on the foot farthest from you, better turn your attention to someone else.

4. Study his hands. If you can see his palms or he's touching his hair or fussing with his clothes, he'd like to get to know you better, but if his hands are in his pockets, clasped together, or touching his ears or nose, he won't be around for long. He's nervous if one hand's holding the other arm; if it's on his hip, however, he's feeling confident. If he's rubbing his eyes or blocking his mouth with his hands, he may be lying or skeptical of what you're saying. What if he's sitting with his index finger pointing upward along his cheek or stroking his chin? Hang around and see what happens—he hasn't made up his mind yet.

HOW TO PARALLEL—PARK

 -- -- -- -- -- -- -- -- -- -- -- -- -- -- -- -- -- -- --

Remember the sheer joy of getting out on the open road for the first time, your combover-sporting, clip-on-sunglasses–wearing driver's ed instructor by your side? He taught you so much: how to turn left at a stoplight, execute a three-point turn, and resist the spell of highway hypnosis. If, however, his parallel-parking lecture has long faded from your memory and you find yourself living in fear of having to drive downtown, it's time to review:

1. Assuming you're parallel-parking on the right, put on your right turn signal, then pull over next to the open parking space and eyeball it to figure out whether you'll fit—the spot should be at least two feet longer than the length of your car.

2. Pull up about two feet away from and parallel to the car in front of the space you want to park in. Your rear bumper should be even with the one on the car next to you.

3. Check traffic behind you, then turn your steering wheel all the way to the right and start to back up into the parking space.

4. When your front wheels are opposite the rear bumper of the car ahead, stop.

5. Turn the steering wheel all the way to the left and back up slowly toward the car behind you. Keep in mind that the front of your car will swing toward the car ahead, so make sure you can clear its back bumper. Also, continue to check in your rear-view mirror so you don't bump the car behind you. If you hit the curb, turn the steering wheel all the way to the right and pull forward as far as you can without bumping the car in front of you, then repeat this step.

6. Straighten your wheels and pull forward toward the center of the parking space, leaving room for the cars in front of and behind you to get out and making sure your wheels are no more than a foot from the curb.

7. If you're parked downhill, turn your steering wheel all the way to the right before shutting off the

engine; if you're parked uphill, turn your steering wheel all the way to the left.

8. Wipe the sweat from your brow, turn off the engine, and put on the parking brake.

HOW TO STAY SAFE IN A TORNADO

When a tornado's headed your way, better grab Toto and seek shelter fast. Twisters have touched down in every state in the union, so no matter where you live, don't blow it—have a plan in place just in case:

1. Prepare for a twister long before one visits a trailer park near you. First, decide on someone out of state to call in case you and anyone you live with get separated. Then designate a shelter spot in your home—the basement, if you have one, or a windowless interior room such as a bathroom, closet, or inner hallway on the first floor if you don't. And finally, put together a disaster supply kit, including first-aid materials, emergency food and water, a can opener, prescription medication, protective clothing, sleeping bags, a battery-powered radio, a flashlight, extra batteries, instructions on how to turn off the utilities in your home if authorities advise you to do so, one hundred dollars in cash, a credit card, extra car

keys, and a photocopy of your driver's license. Store your disaster supply kit in your shelter spot.

2. Stay tuned to the radio or television to keep informed about the onset of a storm. The National Weather Service will issue a tornado watch when tornadoes are possible in your area and a tornado warning when a tornado's been sighted and may be heading your way.

3. If a tornado warning goes into effect, seek shelter immediately:

- If you're at home, go to your shelter spot and get under a piece of sturdy furniture such as a workbench, heavy table, or desk and hold on to it. The goal is to steer clear of any flying debris, a major cause of injuries and deaths during tornadoes.

- If you're outside, move to the basement of a nearby sturdy building or, if there's no time for that, lie in a ditch or low, flat location. Clasp your hands behind your head and use your arms to protect it. Avoid places with wide-span roofs such as auditoriums, cafeterias, or shopping malls.

- If you're in a car or mobile home, get out and head for the safety of a nearby building or, if there's no time, lie flat on the ground. Mobile homes, even when tied down, are extremely vulnerable. And never try to outdrive a tornado—they're capable of changing direction quickly and can lift up a vehicle and flip it through the air.

4. If you're inside a building, listen to the radio to make sure the tornado has passed before you leave your shelter.

5. Help any injured or trapped people around you. If you're in a building and smell gas or chemicals, get out immediately.

6. Listen to your radio for updated emergency information.

HOW TO SET THE TABLE
FOR A DINNER PARTY

If you're having a dinner party for the Donner Party, you can serve your guests any way you please. But if you're hosting a supper soiree for anyone else, you'll want to serve them right by setting your table for a big-deal meal. Forget fretting about finger bowls; this is all you really need to know:

1. Set out your centerpiece. If it's a flower arrangement, make sure it's not so massive as to block guests' views of each other or prevent dishes from being passed easily. And forget the freesia—you don't want any strong-scented blooms competing with the aroma of your apple tart.

2. If you have a set of oversized, decorative plates (known as chargers or service plates), put those out

at each place; if not, put out dinner plates. You'll set your appetizer plates or soup bowls on top of them when you bring out the first course. If you do use chargers, never put any food directly on them, and be sure to replace them with dinner plates before bringing out the main course. Otherwise, you'll simply leave the dinner plates on the table and serve the main course directly on them. If you have bread plates, those go above and to the left of the charger or dinner plate; if you have butter knives, put those across the bread plates parallel to the table edge with the handles on the right.

3. Set your utensils. Forks should go to the left of the plate and knives to the right in the order they'll be used, from outside in; in other words, the fork for the first course is the one farthest to the left and the knife for the first course is the one farthest to the right. Knife blades should face in toward the plate. Spoons go to the right of the knives. A dessert fork and spoon can be set horizontally above the dinner plate (with the spoon on top and the handle facing right and the fork below with the handle facing left).

4. Fold your napkins (preferably cotton or linen) into quarters and then in half into rectangles. Place them lengthwise on the middle of the charger or dinner plate.

5. Put out wine and water glasses. Place the wineglass about half an inch above the main-course knife, then place the water glass slightly above and to the left of that.

6. Handwrite guests' names on place cards (available at stationery stores) and put one above each place setting. Okay, you don't *have* to use them, but they do keep guests from bugging you about where they should sit while you're trying to simultaneously dress the salad, fill the wineglasses, and light the candles. Besides, assigning seats is one of the perks of playing hostess! Boy-girl-boy-girl—but no seating couples next to each other—is the traditional arrangement, though ultimately it's most important that you seat people according to who you think will have the most to chat about. Clear the cards after the first course so they're not in the way, unless you're hosting a big party where most guests don't know one another and you'd be doing them a favor by providing name reminders.

7. Clear all dishes, wineglasses, and condiments from the table before you serve dessert, then put out dessert plates. If you didn't already set out dessert utensils above the dinner plates before your guests arrived, carry them in on a tray at dessert time along with coffee cups and saucers.

HOW TO TREAT POISON IVY

15

So you weren't paying attention in Girl Scouts. For future reference, here's the tip to keep in mind next time you head out for a hike: "Leaves of three, beware of me." In other words, if you see a plant with shiny leaves growing in groups of three, give it a nice, wide berth. Of course, since you've just stepped in some, it's a bit too late for that. What now?

1. Get to water—whether that be a creek, garden hose, whatever—and wash off exposed areas as soon as possible. If you can do this within five minutes, you might be able to prevent the plant's urushiol oil (the culprit that causes the allergic reaction) from bonding with your skin. If possible, follow up with soap and water within a half-hour.

2. Scrub clothes, shoes, pets, camping equipment, garden tools—anything that might have come in contact with the plant. Poison ivy's toxic resin can remain potent on clothing and other items for months, so it's crucial you clean whatever might

have been contaminated so you don't re-expose
yourself later.

3. Treat any rashes that develop with calamine lotion.
   Rashes typically show up within two days, peak
   after five days, and start to disappear after a week
   or ten days. But don't worry: once the urushiol oil
   has been washed off, the rash and blisters won't
   spread to other parts of your body or to another
   person. If you do develop a rash or blisters in a new
   area, it's only because that area took longer to break
   out than the initial exposure.

4. To further combat itching and blistering, try cold
   compresses, cold showers, and/or sprinkling
   oatmeal or baking soda in a lukewarm bath before
   soaking in it.

5. See a doctor if you develop a severe rash, extreme
   swelling, or other symptoms such as fever, nausea,
   or dehydration.

HOW TO CHOOSE A WINE
TO GO WITH YOUR MEAL

16

You've probably heard that red wine goes with red meat and white wine goes with fish and chicken, but though this holds true as a general principle, it's not ironclad. (Besides, what if you're a vegetarian?) Pairing wine with food is a matter of taste—literally—and ultimately, you're the best judge of what works with what. But since that advice doesn't help much when you don't know where to start, and choosing by the coolest-label method isn't very reliable, here's some general guidance:

1. Decide on white or red based on whichever better matches the flavor intensity of your meal. White wines tend to be lighter and more delicately flavored, while red wines are typically more intense. Since light-colored foods (such as chicken, fish, and pasta with cream sauce) are generally mild in flavor, they usually go well with white wines; darker, more strongly flavored foods (such as beef, Portobello mushrooms, and pasta marinara), on the other hand, usually pair better with reds. However, keep

in mind that poultry, seafood, pasta, and other foods can taste pretty neutral on their own—it's often how they're served that gives them a particular flavor. For example, if you're eating chicken baked with lemon, you'd probably want a crisp chardonnay with it, but if you're dining on chicken cacciatore, a Chianti might be a better bet. If whatever you're having happens to have been prepared with a wine-based sauce, you can skip all this and proceed directly to the wine list: just order the same type of wine your meal was cooked with.

2. Balance the weight of the wine with that of the food so one doesn't overwhelm the other. For example, a full-bodied white works well with a heavy dish like fettucini alfredo; however, that same dish would overpower a delicate sauvignon blanc. Popular whites from lightest to heaviest: sauvignon blanc, pinot grigio, Riesling, and chardonnay. Popular reds from lightest to heaviest: merlot, zinfandel, Chianti, pinot noir, cabernet sauvignon, and shiraz (also known as syrah). Keep in mind that these lists are not absolute—a particular zinfandel may be heavier than a particular pinot noir—but they should give you a general idea. If your meal calls for one color wine, but you prefer the other, go ahead and drink the color you like; just get a light red if your meal

would normally be paired with a white, and a heavy white if your meal would normally be paired with a red. For example, if you're taking grilled turkey on a picnic and you want a red wine to go with it, try a merlot.

3. Decide whether you want a wine on the dry or sweet side. Popular reds from dry to sweet: merlot, shiraz (or syrah), cabernet sauvignon, zinfandel, Chianti, pinot noir. Popular whites: chardonnay, viogner, chenin blanc, sauvignon blanc, Riesling, gewurtztraminer. Although sweet foods pair well with sweet wines, understanding the nuances of matching sweet versus dry beyond that is complicated. You're probably best off picking a couple of possibilities based on color and weight and then using your personal sweet or dry preference to finalize your choice. Say you're having salmon roasted in tarragon butter with garlic mashed potatoes on the side. You get it down to a chardonnay or a Riesling, figuring a medium- to full-bodied white would be good, but your preference for a drier wine makes the call: chardonnay it is.

4. Match local cuisine with regional wines when possible—manicotti with Italian wine, paella with Spanish wine, sushi with sake. If the region the dish

is from isn't known for its wines—say you're chowing down on Chinese or Mexican food—that's often a tip-off that an ice-cold beer might be a better accompaniment. (Want wine with those foods anyway? Try a Riesling or another sweet white as a contrast to the spices.)

5. When in doubt, ask for suggestions in your price range. Many wine shop owners and waiters are trained in this stuff, so take advantage of their knowledge. If you're in a restaurant and you'd prefer not to announce your budgetary concerns to everyone in earshot, say "something in this range" and gesture to a few appropriately priced wines on the list instead.

HOW TO FOOL BURGLARS INTO THINKING YOU'RE HOME WHEN YOU'RE NOT

17

Nothing ruins a good vacation like coming home to find your TV, stereo, and international stamp collection missing. Fact is, when it comes to burglar-proofing your house, making it appear that the place is occupied is as important as installing good locks. Here's how to make it look like your nest's not empty:

1. Let your next-door neighbors know you'll be away so they can keep an eye on things and call the cops if they spot anything suspicious. In some areas, you can even tell local police that you'll be out of town and they'll drive by your house periodically to check on it.

2. Arrange for a neighbor or friend to pick up newspapers and mail so people won't know you're away.

3. Have someone mow the grass or shovel snow while you're gone.

4. Keep the drapes closed and use timing devices to turn lamps, radios, and TVs on and off. (Speaking of which, you might also want to use timers when you're out for the evening or during the day while you're at work.)

5. In case your house gets broken into anyway, take an inventory of all your valuables. Write down appliance descriptions and serial numbers so you'll know exactly what's missing. To be on the even safer side, get an engraver (available at hardware stores) and engrave your driver's license number onto any items of value, so if they're stolen and then recovered by police, they can be easily returned to you. If you own expensive jewelry you don't wear often, put it in a safe-deposit box. And whatever you do, don't keep large wads of cash lying around the house (or even tucked under your mattress).

HOW TO MAKE YOUR PERFUME LAST

18

If your scent never seems to make it through soup and salad (never mind the good-night kiss), it's time to learn to make it linger longer. If you're shopping for a new perfume, keep in mind that stronger, more dramatic fragrances, such as orientals and woodsy scents, won't fade as fast as your average light floral. But no matter what perfume you prefer, make it last longer by following these tips:

1. Before applying perfume, use at least one more product scented with your fragrance, such as body lotion, shower gel, soap, or powder. Layering fragrance gives it extra staying power.

2. Rub a little petroleum jelly or unscented lotion (or better yet, lotion scented with your fragrance) into your wrists and neck, then put a little on your ankles and behind your knees. Because perfume disappears faster on dry skin, moisturizing it first helps make the scent last.

3. Apply perfume on pulse points on your wrist and neck, since they tend to be warm and radiate fragrance well. And because scent rises, put a little on your ankles and behind your knees.

4. If you know you'll be out late, take your perfume with you so you can reapply it, since fragrance typically fades after three to four hours and even sooner if it's cold out or you live at a high altitude. But don't try to make it last longer by spraying on more than usual; drenching yourself in fragrance will only cause everyone around you to gag. No one should be able to smell your scent until they're close enough to touch you.

5. Store perfume in a cool, dry place. The glass bottle may sparkle in the sunlight on your dresser, but heat and light weaken a fragrance and can spoil its scent.

HOW TO WRITE A CONDOLENCE NOTE

19

When someone dies, many people are so nervous they'll say something wrong that they end up saying nothing at all. Don't make that mistake—if ever a friend needed to hear from you, it's now. And don't bother trying to sound like a Hallmark card; if your sympathy note is overly formal or flowery, it'll just come across as impersonal. Instead, keep in mind that the most important thing is simply to give comfort and express your appreciation or love for the person who's gone. Here are some guidelines on what to include:

1. Open your letter by acknowledging the loss and saying how sorry you are.

2. Recall special memories or qualities of the deceased. The point of your letter should be to celebrate that person's life rather than be morbid about the loss. Write about good times together, how the person influenced your life, even a funny story. The mourner and the family will appreciate your reminiscences. If you didn't know the person

yourself, mention something special you've heard about him or her. Don't say you understand what the mourner is going through, try to make sense of the death, or mention anything like "It's time to get on with your life." And don't overemphasize how much you personally feel the loss—this letter shouldn't focus on your grief.

3. If you know the mourner well, offer help. Rather than putting the burden on the bereaved with the generic "If there's anything I can do, let me know," suggest something specific—running errands, making and sending over meals, babysitting, walking the dog. Although the mourner may not take you up on your offer right now, he or she might really appreciate your help in the future.

4. End your letter with warm words such as "You're in my thoughts," "You have my deepest sympathy," or "My prayers are with you."

20

Yeah, yeah, you *could* start a campfire by rubbing two sticks together, but why would you want to? If you're going camping or even on a long day hike, carry matches as well as a few fire-starter cubes—available at camping, grocery, and hardware stores—in a waterproof case or Ziploc baggie. That way, you're guaranteed warmth, something to purify water and cook with, and a means to signal rescuers if you need it (not to mention a way to make s'mores). Now, on to that campfire, girl:

1. Gather everything you need: tinder (highly flammable items such as dried bark, dead moss, and newspaper), kindling (sticks, twigs, and pine needles), and fuel (larger pieces of wood). Make sure you select dry, dead stuff or it won't burn very well. Wet weather? You may have to split open a fallen log to get at dry wood. If you're camping in a national park that allows fires, keep in mind you'll have to bring your own firewood rather than collecting it around your campsite. Firewood is

available in some supermarkets; you can also look under "Firewood" in the Yellow Pages to find places to buy it. You may also be able to get it in stores inside the park—check the park's Web site if you're not sure.

2. Pick a place to start your fire. If there's a designated fire ring, use it; if not, choose an area not too close to tents, trees, and dried grass.

3. If there's no fire ring available, dig a pit about a foot deep and a few feet wide for your fire, remembering to keep the piece of topsoil so you can put it back later.

4. Put the tinder (along with a fire-starter cube, if you've got one) in a small stack, making sure you leave lots of holes for air to circulate.

5. Form a tepee structure with the kindling over the tinder stack.

6. Strike a match and light the fire by igniting the tinder at the base.

7. Once the fire is burning really well, add the fuel wood to keep it going. If you want to cook with your

fire, let the tepee burn down—smoldering wood actually cooks better than flames.

8. Before you leave the site or retire for the night, be certain you put out the fire completely. Allow it to burn down to ash, then throw plenty of water on it and sift through the embers with a stick to make sure the fire is totally extinguished.

9. Sprinkle the cooled ashes across a wide area.

10. Scatter any unused firewood.

11. If you dug a fire pit, put the chunk of topsoil back over it and pat down.

HOW TO GET A FAMILY
HEIRLOOM APPRAISED

21

Have a hunch that the hutch you inherited from Grandma came over on the *Mayflower* and could fetch a mint? Get an appraiser and you'll get your answer. Here's how to find out an antique's true value:

1. Find a reputable appraiser. The International Society of Appraisers (isa-appraisers.org), the American Society of Appraisers (appraisers.org), and the Appraisers Association of America (appraisersassoc.org) all have online directories that you can use to search for an appraiser in your area. And it never hurts to ask around—family, friends, and coworkers might also have recommendations.

2. Choose someone with expertise in the type of object you need appraised. There's a range of appraisal specialties—folk art, European furniture, books and manuscripts, and gems and jewelry, just to name a few—and appraisers typically focus on a

particular area. However, if you've got a bunch of stuff you want appraised (say, paintings, rugs, photographs, and jewelry), you can start with a generalist who'll consult with or refer you to the right specialists.

3. Ask about the appraiser's credentials. Formal training is a must. Membership in an appraisal association is also key because it means the appraiser is subject to a professional code of ethics and should be in the know about the latest appraisal laws and procedures.

4. Tell the appraiser why you need the appraisal. Although you obviously might want to know how much something's worth in case you want to sell it, you may also wonder for insurance, charitable donation, or estate tax purposes. And depending on the reason for the appraisal, the same item can have different appraised values.

5. Find out how much the appraisal will cost. The appraiser's work involves inspecting the object in person (a photo isn't enough for an accurate appraisal), researching it, and putting together a written report. Will the appraiser charge an hourly rate, flat fee, or per-item fee? Never agree to an

arrangement that has you paying a percentage of the appraised value of the object, since this would be a conflict of interest for the appraiser.

6. Get an appraisal report. The key elements a report should contain: the reason for the appraisal, the methodology and resources used to develop the appraisal, a thorough description of the object, how the object was acquired, the appraiser's qualifications, a statement that the appraiser has no financial interest in the object, the date the object was inspected, and the appraiser's signature.

Little Spot is doggone adorable, all right, although he may seem less so when you're cleaning up the little spot he left on the living-room rug. Want to teach Spotty to go potty? As long as he's at least nine weeks old, you can. Here's how:

1. Get help if you need it. Ideally, you should be home most of the time so you can focus on training your puppy, but if that's not possible, at least make sure he's not left alone all day. If you have to be out of the house for more than a couple of hours every weekday, for example, drop him off at a doggie day care center or arrange to have a dog walker take him for regularly scheduled walks (ask your vet and friends with pooches for recommendations).

2. Go to a pet store and buy a dog crate just big enough for your puppy to stand up and turn around in.

3. Give your puppy food and water at the same times every day. If the input's on a regular schedule, the output should be too.

4. Designate a spot outdoors as your puppy's bathroom, and take him to it every hour or so. You should also take him out right after naps, meals, and play sessions. As soon as you get outside, take him straight there; wait to go for a walk or play with him till after he's finished.

5. Keep your pooch in the crate for up to two hours at a time. Because dogs won't make a mess where they sleep, being in the crate will help teach your pup to hold it. Never use the crate as punishment!

6. Whenever your pup's not in the crate, keep a sharp eye on him and shut off the room you're in by closing the door or blocking it with boxes or baby gates. Watch for signs that he needs to go—if he suddenly starts sniffing the floor or walking in circles, take him out pronto.

7. Anytime your pooch is relieving himself outdoors, say "do your business" and praise him when he's finished. The idea is that eventually all you'll have to

do is say "do your business" and he'll go on command.

8. As soon as your puppy has finished relieving himself, congratulate him in an enthusiastic, high voice. Lots of praise is key to successful house-training, so lay it on thick.

9. If you catch your puppy going when he's still inside, stop him by grabbing his collar and telling him "No!" in a gruff voice. Then take him to his designated spot outside. If he finishes up there, praise him and give him a treat.

10. Anytime your dog has an accident you discover after the fact, even if it's just a minute later, don't reprimand him—he won't understand, so you'll only confuse and scare him. Just clean up the mess and then take any rags or paper towels you used and put them in his designated outdoor spot. The smell will reinforce that that's where he's supposed to go, not inside.

11. Whenever you have to leave your puppy alone for more than two hours, close the door or use boxes or baby gates to shut him in a laundry room,

bathroom, or another small room with enough space for his crate, his food and water, an area to play in, and a separate area covered with newspapers where he can relieve himself. However, keep in mind that letting your dog do his business inside on a regular basis prolongs the house-training process and may teach your pup a lifelong habit that could make reading the newspaper at home significantly less pleasant in the future—after all, you know what they say about teaching an old dog new tricks.

12. Be patient and consistent with your training. Your dog will have accidents, and cleaning them up off your carpet is no picnic. But don't expect instant results. It'll probably take several months before little Spot's completely house-trained.

HOW TO GET BUMPED FROM A FLIGHT
ON PURPOSE

How'd you like to get paid a hundred dollars an hour to sit around and read *USA Today*? That's basically what happens when you get bumped from a flight—in exchange for voluntarily giving up your seat, you get a free ticket or travel voucher often worth big bucks. Most airlines oversell their flights to compensate for ticket holders who just don't show up, but when too many expected no-shows *do* show, the airline has to bump some passengers to the next available flight—and offer those passengers compensation. So unless you need to be somewhere to give a sales presentation or donate a kidney (or you hate reading), getting bumped can be a great deal. Here's how to make your chances of future free travel soar:

1. If you have more than one airport you could fly into or out of, go with common business routes and popular tourist destinations whenever possible.
   Nonstop flights on routes with a limited number of daily departures are also good.

2. Reserve a ticket well in advance so you can get on a flight that will hopefully become oversold later. To boost your bumping odds, pick a peak time, such as around holidays, early Monday mornings, and Fridays and Sundays around 5 PM. Choosing the last flight of the day may also pay off, since fewer people are likely to volunteer to get bumped when an overnight stay's involved. If more than one flight works for you, call the airline, ask which plane has the fewest seats left, and then buy a ticket on it.

3. Call your travel agent or the airline the day before your flight to ask if it looks like it'll be a full plane. If so, and someone's planning to pick you up at your destination, call to let her know that you may get bumped and ask her to check her messages before leaving for the airport. If you're worried that your later arrival could be an inconvenience, offer to take a taxi or rent a car. Most likely, the cost of a cab or car will be much lower than what you'd get in exchange for being bumped.

4. Pack any valuables in your carry-on luggage. While this is always a good idea, it's especially important if you think you might be bumped, since the airline may simply set your checked suitcases to one side at baggage claim and leave them there till your

arrival. Or you could always just travel light and pack carry-ons only.

5. If you're really organized, bring along a list of alternate flight times so if you're bumped, you can tell the agent which flight you'd like. Before you leave, check the airline's Web site for schedules and print out the departure times to your destination for your day of travel. (You can also get an airline's printed schedule for all their flights at the airport, so if you travel with a particular carrier a lot, you might want to ask for one at their ticket counter the next time you fly.) It's not out of the realm of possibility that you could be bumped from a connecting flight and then score a free ticket as well as a seat on a nonstop flight that gets you to where you're going *ahead of* your original flight.

6. Since airlines bump people on a first-come, first-served basis, get to the airport with plenty of time to spare, and never wait for an announcement asking for volunteers to give up their seats. Instead, as soon as you get to the gate, ask the agent if the flight's overbooked and, if it is, let him know you'd like to volunteer. If he thinks he may need you, he'll take your ticket and tell you to listen for an announcement after the plane has finished

boarding. At that point, if enough ticket holders still haven't shown up for the flight, you'll simply be told to get on board. However, if you're lucky, the agent may give you a small voucher ($25, say) just for volunteering, even if you don't get bumped after all. More good news: since you're boarding last, it's also possible you'll get an empty seat in first or business class without having to pay extra for it.

7. If the airline does need volunteers, find out what compensation you'll get. If a free ticket or travel voucher is being offered, check on any restrictions, such as expiration or blackout dates. You should also ask if you'll be guaranteed a seat on the next available flight and what will happen if that flight's canceled. If you have to stay overnight, will the airline pay for your hotel, ground transportation, and meals? Such expenses are sometimes covered, but if they aren't, getting bumped might not be worth it unless you'll get a really pricey travel voucher or ticket in return.

8. Politely negotiate for more if you're not satisfied with what the airline is offering. If you know the airline is scrambling to find volunteers (you're flying on the Wednesday night before Thanksgiving, for example, and the airport's teeming with travelers),

you might even ask for compensation worth a hundred or two hundred dollars more than what's being offered. That said, if half the plane stormed the gate agents when they asked for volunteers, you'd probably be better off either taking or leaving what's on offer. Since the agents may choose volunteers willing to get bumped for the lowest price, if you try to drive too hard a bargain, you might drive yourself right out of that free ticket or voucher.

9. If you do get bumped and have to wait a few hours until the next flight, ask about airport restaurant meal vouchers, phone cards, and access to the airline's lounge. You may also want to ask whether you can get on an earlier plane on a different carrier. Although the airline is unlikely to do that, it has happened.

10. If you've got a ton of time on your hands and your next flight is overbooked as well, volunteer to be bumped again. Bumping often causes a domino effect, especially during busy travel periods when overflow passengers are being added to already full flights, so you could land a second (or even third!) ticket or travel voucher before ever taking off.

HOW TO CHANGE A FLAT TIRE

24-- -- -- -- -- -- -- -- -- -- -- -- -- -- -- -- -- --

Flat is fine for abs and pancakes, but not so terrific when it comes to tires. If you're cruising down the highway, looking for adventure, and your ride suddenly turns bumpy, chances are you've got a flat. Better pull over and fix it so you can get on the road again:

1. Park the car on firm, level ground away from traffic. Shut off the engine and put the car in park if you have an automatic transmission; if you have a manual transmission, put it in reverse.

2. Set the parking brake.

3. Turn on your hazard lights.

4. To be extra safe and prevent the car from rolling, find two big rocks and put them in front of and behind the tire diagonally opposite the one you're changing.

5. Open your trunk and get out your spare tire, jack, and lug wrench. If you have a van or SUV, the spare may be mounted under the rear of your vehicle.

6. If there's a hubcap on the flat tire, pry it off with a screwdriver or the flat end of the lug wrench to expose the lug nuts. Loosen the nuts on the tire with the lug wrench, but don't remove them all the way.

7. Following the instructions in your owner's manual, place the jack under the car as recommended and jack up your vehicle until the flat tire is clear of the ground. Warning: never get under the car when it's jacked up.

8. Remove the lug nuts completely, lift off the flat tire, and set it aside.

9. Put on the spare tire, positioning it so its holes are aligned with the bolts on the wheel hub. Make sure the tire is firmly against the hub, then replace and tighten all the lug nuts as tightly as you can by hand.

10. Lower your car to the ground.

11. Use the lug wrench to fully tighten the lug nuts in a crisscross pattern—first tightening one nut, then the one directly opposite it, and so on.

12. Put your damaged tire, the tools, and the hubcap (if there is one) in your trunk. Be aware that most spare tires are designed to serve only as temporary replacements, so driving farther or faster than recommended on one can be dangerous. Drive slowly, and get your regular tire repaired or replaced and put back on your car as soon as possible.

HOW TO BUY A DIAMOND

25

Diamonds may be a girl's best friend, but that doesn't mean all jewelers are. Sure, you can stroll into a jewelry shop, point to the biggest, sparkliest rock in the display case, and waltz out with that sizeable ring on your finger (and an even more sizeable dent in your bank account). But it's smarter to do research first and shop later so you know what you're getting and don't get ripped off. Whether you're buying a ring for yourself or "helping" the man in your life pick out one for you, it pays to learn the lingo before you walk into a jewelry store and select a stone:

1. Study up on the four "C"s, which determine a diamond's quality and value.

- *Carat:* Equal to .20 grams, the carat is the standard unit of weight for diamonds. Diamond weights are also sometimes measured in points: One carat equals one hundred points, so a fifty-point diamond would weigh one-half carat (and be about the size of a small pea).

- *Color:* When it comes to a diamond's color, less is more. With the exception of natural fancy colors, such as yellow, blue, purple, pink, and red, the colorless grade is the most valuable. Most diamonds have at least a trace of yellow or brown body color.

- *Clarity:* The clarity scale is a measure of the severity of a diamond's imperfections on the outside (called blemishes) and the inside (called inclusions). A "cleaner" stone with fewer flaws makes for more sparkle—and a higher price tag.

- *Cut:* Cut refers to the number, placement, and shape of the flat, polished planes (called facets) that create a finished diamond—and contribute directly to its sparkle factor. The better the cut, the more brilliant and valuable the stone.

2. Ask friends, family, and coworkers for referrals to reliable independent jewelry stores—they often have better prices than chains. Stick to reputable jewelers who are knowledgeable and helpful and have fair return and repair policies.

3. Determine your budget and stick to it. Don't get too dazzled by a rock you can't afford.

4. At the jeweler, check out all the diamond shapes available and decide which one you like best. There are seven main types: round, oval, heart, princess (square), emerald (rectangular), marquise (oval with pointed ends), and pear (which is shaped more like a teardrop than a pear, but anyway). You can also choose from lots of different settings for your diamond, but some are more appropriate than others for specific shapes; ask your jeweler about the best options.

5. Once you've settled on the shape, look for a loose stone rather than one that's already mounted. That way, you can inspect it completely for imperfections with the jeweler's loupe (a magnifying tool).

6. Make sure the stone you want comes with a diamond grading certificate from an independent appraisal lab—the big four are the Gemological Institute of America (GIA), the American Gemological Society (AGS), the European Gemological Laboratories (EGL), and the International Gemological Institute (IGI)—so you know you're getting what you pay for.

7. Negotiate. Most retailers mark up the cost of their rocks by at least one hundred percent, so never pay

full sticker price unless you've shopped around and know it's a great deal. The simple words "What's the best price you can give me on this diamond?" could save you a bundle.

8. Once the stone's been set, check the diagram of its imperfections (which should be included with the diamond grading certificate) to ensure the diamond you're picking up is the same one you purchased.

HOW TO HEM A SKIRT

26

Want to turn that full-length bridesmaid's dress into something you might *really* wear again? Like, you know, in the real world, where you don't get many invitations for galas requiring floor-sweeping gowns? Shorten it! Ditto for any skirt you like, but would like even better if there were less of it. Luckily, hemming a skirt is pretty simple, and by performing the skirt surgery yourself, you'll save substantial cashola. Here's how:

1. Put on the skirt and have a friend pin it up in front to the length you want. The pins should run parallel to the floor.

2. With the skirt still on, ask your friend to measure with a yardstick from the floor up to the edge of the fold you've just made.

3. Have your friend pin up the rest of the skirt to that measurement, using the yardstick as a guide and pinning as she goes.

4. Press this new hemline with an iron to form a crease.

5. Unpin the hem and measure two inches longer than the crease line (this is called the hem allowance). Use a pencil or fabric chalk to mark the fabric as you measure around the skirt, then cut off any fabric beyond the two-inch line.

6. Turn the skirt inside out and fold the raw, cut edge over so it meets the crease line. Iron.

7. Fold it over again, creating a double one-inch fold, then pin it in place and iron again. (The reason for making this double fold is to avoid sewing directly on the raw edge of the material, which can fray and unravel.) Don't remove the pins.

8. Thread your needle with thread that's the same shade or slightly darker than the color of your skirt and knot it.

9. Starting at a side seam, pull the needle through the top edge of the hem on the inside of the skirt. Your first stitch should just catch the fabric on the outside of the skirt with a tiny bit of thread, since this is the side that will show.

10. Make your next stitch, on the inside of your skirt, no more than a half-inch wide.

11. Continue making tiny stitches on the outside and larger stitches on the inside.

12. When you're about a quarter of the way around the skirt, knot the thread and start a new one. Do this again at the halfway and three-quarters points. That way, if the thread rips, the whole hem won't come down.

HOW TO CRACK A COCONUT

Consuming fruit doesn't usually require breaking out your toolbox—unless, of course, you're craving coconut. But before you get cracking, make sure you choose a choice specimen: pick the one that seems heaviest for its size, sounds like it has the most liquid sloshing around inside, and has no fermentation smell or sign of moisture near the two or three eyes on the end of the shell. You can keep a coconut in a cool spot on your counter for a couple of weeks, but once it's opened, keep it in the fridge and eat it within a few days. Here's how to get your coconut to come out of its shell:

1. Puncture the eyes of the coconut with a hammer and nail or screwdriver (clean the nail or screwdriver first with hot water and dishwashing liquid).

2. Holding the coconut over a bowl or cup, drain the watery liquid, which you can drink as is. Just remember that although this stuff is often referred to as coconut milk, it's not the same as the

commercial coconut milk commonly called for in recipes, which is an infusion of grated coconut meat and boiling water.

3. Roast the coconut in the oven at 375 degrees Fahrenheit for twenty to twenty-five minutes or until it starts to crack.

4. Take it out of the oven and tap the shell all around to release the white meat inside.

5. Set it crack side up, cover with a towel, and smack the shell with a hammer. It should break easily.

6. Remove the meat in pieces with a small, sharp knife.

7. Eat and enjoy! If you were planning to use the meat to bake with, you should know that it's not the same as the commercial coconut commonly called for in recipes (sound familiar?), which is sweetened. However, you can remove the thin brown skin from the meat with a vegetable peeler, grate the meat, and add it to salads and curries if you want.

HOW TO GET THE SMELL OF SMOKE

OUT OF A ROOM

 -

Smoke may get in your eyes, but that doesn't mean it has to stay in your house. If you're expecting chain-smoking guests, take preventive measures before they arrive: light scented candles around the room and dust the bottom of ashtrays with baking soda to minimize the smell and prevent cigarette butts from smoldering. Party's over, but you're still sniffing smoke? Try this:

1. If the weather allows, open windows to air the room out (duh!).

2. For a quick fix, soak a dish towel with vinegar, wring it out, then walk through the room and wave it around. If you have more time, leave a couple of small dishes of vinegar out for a few days.

3. If curtains, fabric slipcovers, or pillowcases that you don't want to wash have absorbed the smoky smell, put them in the dryer on a cool setting for five minutes with a few sheets of fabric softener.

Don't worry if you don't know a daily double from a trifecta. It doesn't even matter if all you know about horseracing is that the Kentucky Derby is, um, in Kentucky. Learning a few basics is all you need to enjoy a day at the races—and maybe even fatten your wallet while you're at it. Feeling lucky? Here's how to place a bet:

1. Learn how the betting system works. Basically, when you place a bet, you're betting against everyone else making the same type of bet in the same race. Every track has an official handicapper who evaluates stuff like the horse's past race performances and then assigns odds, or the probability of winning, to each horse. People can use these odds as a guide for placing their own bets, but ultimately it's the overall pool of bettors that determines the actual odds. With this system, the more people holding a winning ticket for a particular race, the less each person wins. Which is why if you bet on a long-shot horse—that is, one that few people have

bet on—you can rake in the bucks if it does well. In other words, the higher the risk, the greater the payoff.

2. Check out the horses before choosing which one to bet on. Pick up a copy of the day's official program at the track to find out basic information about the horses in each race, including their betting odds from the track's handicapper. Odds of 15–1 (which would show up as just "15" on the program; the "to 1" is understood) would make a horse a long shot to win, while a horse with 2–1 odds (represented by "2" on the program) would likely be considered the favorite. If it turns out you love racing, you can learn how to properly handicap horses later, but for the sake of getting started, an easy strategy is to bet on the favorite, since it wins about a third of the time. It's also fun to watch the horses as they're paraded right before their race. That way, you can see them up close and place your bet based on how they look, as well as their odds.

3. Decide what type of bet you want to make. There are a bunch of options, but the simplest are win, place, and show. If you make a win bet, your horse must come in first in the race for you to collect; with a place bet, you collect if your horse comes in first

or second; and if you bet to show, you collect if your horse finishes first, second, or third.

4. Figure out how much money you want to bet. The minimum is usually $2 in cash. Don't forget the fundamental rule of gambling: never bet more than you can afford to lose.

5. Go to the betting window at least five or ten minutes before the race and tell the clerk which race you're betting on, how much money you're betting, the type of bet (win, place, or show), and the horse you're betting on (giving its program number rather than name). So, for example, you could say, "In the third race, two dollars to win on the number seven horse." To keep things straight, you might even want to write down the information on the program before you go to the window.

6. Pay the clerk the amount you've bet and get your ticket.

7. Double-check that all the information is correct before you walk away from the window, because once the race begins, you're stuck with that ticket, no matter what.

8. Put the ticket somewhere you won't lose it—you'll need it to collect if you win.

9. Look for the results of the race on a TV monitor or what's known as a tote board (the main one is located in the center of the track, usually across from the finish line). And never throw away what you assume is a losing ticket until the official race results have been posted; sometimes a horse can be disqualified after the race, changing the results and making your ticket worth something after all.

10. If you've made a winning bet, take your ticket to any window after the race is declared official and collect. If you're unsure whether you've got a winning ticket, have it checked at the window. Just avoid cashing winning tickets right before another race; many people like to wait until the last few minutes before a race to place their bets, so cashing in during that time is unlikely to endear you to everyone in line behind you.

The words "used car" may conjure up an image of a fast-talking sales guy trying to unload a lemon that'll break down the minute you drive off the lot, but buying a pre-owned vehicle doesn't have to leave a sour taste in your mouth. Here's an overview of the process and what you should keep in mind:

1. Narrow your choices. Obviously, you should consider price, but you should also think about the type of car that will best fit your needs. If you go wind-surfing up the coast on weekends, for example, you'll probably want a bigger car than someone who has to parallel park in the city every day. If you need help figuring out which models to consider, try the decision-making tools on AutoTrader.com, Edmunds.com, and Kelley Blue Book (kbb.com).

2. Investigate the price, repair record, maintenance costs, and safety and mileage ratings for the cars

you're interested in. Good general sites to consult include Carpoint.com, Cars.com, AutoTrader.com, Edmunds.com, and Kelley Blue Book (kbb.com). For repair records, look at the charts in the annual auto issues of *Consumer Reports* at your local library. For safety information, check out the crash tests on the National Highway Traffic Safety Administration (nhtsa.org) and The Insurance Institute for Highway Safety and the Highway Loss Data Institute (hwysafety.org) sites.

3. If you need help paying for the car, research your financing options and get approval for a loan *before* you start to shop. Common sources of financing are banks, auto dealers, credit unions, and finance companies. Just as you'd shop around for a car, shop around for a loan in order to get the best deal. One easy way to start researching your options is to check out the finance section of major automotive Web sites (see step two).

4. Start shopping. Used vehicles are primarily sold by individuals, new car dealers, and franchise and independent used car dealers, though you may also want to look into rental and leasing companies. Keep in mind that buying from a dealership can be more pricey than buying from an individual, but with a

dealer you usually get at least a thirty-day warranty. Many dealers also offer certified used cars, which means they've been reconditioned, passed a thorough inspection, and are backed by a manufacturer's warranty. If you'd prefer to buy through an individual, check out your local paper's classifieds or search for cars in your area (you'll be asked for your zip code) on sites such as AutoTrader.com, Carpoint.com, and Cars.com.

5. Inspect any car you're interested in. You can find a detailed inspection checklist on the Web by doing a search for "used car inspection checklist," but here are the basics: Is the tread on the tires worn down? Are any of the body parts a different color? Are there any uneven gaps between the doors or along the hood? Are there any fluid leaks under the hood or under the car? Do you have difficulty opening the doors or trunk? Are the lights, controls, heater, air conditioner, or sound system broken? Does the engine make any funny noises? If you answered yes to any of these questions, consider whether you really want to buy this car.

6. Test-drive the car on a range of road conditions, including hills, highways, and stop-and-go traffic. How are the acceleration and braking? Does the car

make any strange squeaks or rattles? And don't forget the comfort factor—how do you feel driving the car? Is there enough head room and leg room? Do the seats, steering wheel, and mirrors adjust comfortably?

7. Find out as much as you can about the car's history. Ask for the car's maintenance records from the owner or dealer. If the owner hasn't kept records, suggest checking with the owner's repair shop to see if they have them. Make sure it's had regular oil changes, and watch out for any major repairs—they could be a red flag. For about twenty dollars, you can run a vehicle history report with a company called CarFax (carfax.com) to find out if the car has any hidden problems such as accident or flood damage, odometer fraud, or a failed state emissions inspection.

8. Ask the seller to accompany you to get the car inspected by a mechanic *you* select. An inspection should cost a hundred dollars or less.

9. Negotiate the best deal you can. Never automatically agree to the initial asking price. If your mechanic has recommended any repairs, ask the seller to make those fixes before you buy the car

or knock the cost of the repairs off the overall asking price.

10. Finalize the deal. If you're buying from a dealership, try to get any option additions and repair work you've both agreed on done before you sign the contract. You'll also need to provide proof of insurance. If you're purchasing from an individual, check with your state's department of motor vehicles for the details on all the legal stuff like title transfer and smog certification. Then, two copies of a bill of sale should be drawn up, including your name, address, and phone number and that of the seller; the car's make, model, year, Vehicle Identification Number (VIN), and mileage; the full sale price and how the car was paid for; and a statement that says the car was sold in "as is" condition or spells out any repair work the seller has agreed to do. You and the seller should sign and date both copies and each of you should receive one.

HOW TO BREW COFFEE

31

Maybe coffee isn't your cup of tea, but you want to know how to make it for guests. Or maybe you've got a four-cup-a-day habit, but you've been getting your fix at Starbucks. Either way, if you've got a tablespoon and an electric-drip coffeemaker (such as a Mr. Coffee), you can brew great java at home. Here's how:

1. Buy quality beans from a specialty coffee shop that sells freshly roasted coffee. The fresher the coffee and the more recently it's been roasted, the better the taste, so ask what's been roasted that day and buy that. Old roasted coffee loses flavor from prolonged exposure to air, light, and moisture.

2. Get whole beans. Pre-ground coffee starts to lose flavor in as little as a day, so it's best to start with a bag of whole beans and grind as you go. Don't have a coffee grinder? Use your blender instead.

3. Buy just a small amount of coffee beans at a time, preferably only as much as you can use up in a week or two. Again, freshness is key.

4. Store your coffee in an airtight container in a cool, dry, dark cabinet. The idea is to avoid air, light, heat, and moisture, since they rob coffee of its flavor. If you've bought more than you can drink in two weeks, put the amount you don't think you'll use by then in a Ziploc bag and suck the air out of the bag with a straw while you seal it. Then put that bag in a second Ziploc bag, suck the air out of that one, and freeze. And once you remove it from the freezer, keep it out: defrosting and then refreezing coffee compromises its quality.

5. Measure your coffee. Although the amount you use is a matter of taste, a good rule of thumb is one tablespoon of ground coffee per coffee cup or two tablespoons per standard eight-ounce mug.

6. Grind only as many beans as you can use at one time, and do it right before you brew a pot. About twenty seconds in an electric grinder should give you the ideal coarseness for a drip coffeemaker.

7. If you don't have a reusable filter, put a paper one in your filter holder.

8. Add the ground coffee to the filter.

9. Since the water level markings on coffeemakers vary so much, ignore them; instead, figure out how much water to use by filling the cups or mugs you'll be drinking from. Although tap water is okay, using filtered water will generally give you better-tasting coffee.

10. Bring your water to a boil on the stove, then let it sit for a couple of minutes. Although you may have heard that you're supposed to use cold water to make coffee, water at 195 to 200 degrees actually does the best job extracting the flavor from the grounds, and since most coffeemakers don't heat coffee enough on their own, using already hot water is the only way to ensure a steaming cup of joe.

11. Pour the water into the back of your coffeemaker.

12. Brew only as much as you can drink in the next fifteen minutes; after that, coffee tends to taste bitter and burned. If you want to make one big pot

and drink it a little at a time, transfer your hot coffee to a thermos to keep it tasting fresh for up to an hour.

13. As soon as you've poured all your coffee, take the coffeepot off the burner so it doesn't burn; even if the coffeemaker is turned off, the burner will still be hot.

14. Rinse your coffeepot (and the reusable filter, if it has one) with hot water after each use, since traces of old coffee grounds will make future pots taste bitter. Wash the coffeepot and the plastic filter holder thoroughly with dishwashing soap at least once a week to remove oils left over from old coffee.

HOW TO FIX A CLOGGED TOILET

 -

Nobody likes a close encounter with a clogged commode,
but unfortunately, hoping the problem will magically disappear isn't very effective. Instead, take the plunge and fix it
the old-fashioned way:

1. Don't flush the toilet again or you could cause the
   bowl to overflow. And don't be tempted to try a
   liquid clog remover designed for drains—not only
   will it not work, but it could crack your toilet bowl.
   Instead, get a plunger and position it over the drain
   hole in the toilet. If you have a force-cup plunger
   (one with an inner cup in the suction part), use
   that; they're more effective on toilet clogs than
   standard plungers. But whichever type you're
   using, the idea is to plunge up and down quickly,
   keeping the plunger underwater and lifting it only
   an inch or so on each upstroke. You'll know the
   clog has been removed once water starts flowing
   down the bowl.

2. If plunging doesn't clear the clog, try a closet auger. Also known as a toilet auger, this plumbing tool is basically a long piece of cable inside a protective tube with a handle. (If you find yourself fresh out of augers, you can pick one up at a hardware store.) Feed the end of the cable into the toilet, being careful not to scratch the bowl, and use a cranking and pulling action to snag the offending obstruction and break up the blockage.

3. If the toilet is still stopped up, it might need to be removed from the floor and turned upside down so the obstruction can be forced out from the top or bottom. In other words, it's time to get on the horn and call a plumber.

HOW TO CARVE A TURKEY

33 –––––––––––––––––––––––––––––––––––

You've stuffed the Butterball, candied the yams, whipped up the triple-layer Jell-O salad, and even managed to sneak in a few minutes of the game. Now there's just one last thing to do before your guests flock to your table to gobble down dinner—carve the turkey. Here's the simplest way to make the cut:

1. Once the turkey's out of the oven, remove the stuffing, then let the bird stand uncovered for fifteen to thirty minutes to allow the juices to saturate the meat.

2. Get out a sharp carving knife; a dull blade will shred the meat when you start cutting.

3. Put the turkey on a carving board, breast side up.

4. Slice through the skin where each leg is attached to the breast, then pull the entire leg out and back, using the knifepoint to detach it. Transfer the leg to

the side of the carving board and separate the drumstick and thigh by cutting through the joint. If it's a big bird, cut pieces of meat from both the drumsticks and thighs by slicing parallel to the bone. For smaller birds, just put drumsticks and thighs on a platter for people to eat as is.

5. Pry each wing away from the body with a fork or your hand until the joint is exposed, then cut through it. Wings can be eaten whole or cut into pieces.

6. Carve the breast meat. Begin halfway up the breast and make long, thin, slanting slices, parallel to the breastbone. Work your way up, and when you've finished one side of the bird, turn it around and repeat the process on the other side.

7. Transfer the meat to a platter.

HOW TO FEND OFF AN ATTACKER

 –

When it comes to protecting yourself against an assailant, your first thought may be to learn jiujitsu or buy pepper spray for your purse. But since most crimes against women are committed by people they know, your best defense is trusting your gut and getting out of any situation that doesn't feel right. If you do find yourself in scary circumstances, here's what to do:

1. Use your intuition and know what your personal boundaries are. If something doesn't feel safe, get up and leave. And if you don't want to spend time with someone or have him touch you, say no. Don't hesitate because you're afraid of being rude or hurting someone's feelings.

2. If you are attacked, run away if you can. If you have to get physical to escape, strike the attacker in areas he's most vulnerable: his eyes, groin, throat, and knees.

3. If he fights back, continue to concentrate on exposed areas rather than focusing all your effort on what he's doing. For example, if he grabs your arm, don't waste your energy trying to break his grip; instead, use whatever else you have available (for example, your feet) to hit his knees or another vulnerable part of his body. In other words, target your strengths against your attacker's weaknesses.

4. If you spot someone nearby, yell, "Hey, you in the red shirt, call 911 now!" People usually respond better to a direct instruction than a general "Help!" If you can't see anyone, but you're in an apartment or anywhere else within earshot of others, yell "Fire!" When people hear "Help!", they may think it's just joking around or feel reluctant to get involved, but "Fire!" will usually get their attention and spur them to investigate.

5. Do whatever you have to do to prevent the attacker from getting you in a car and taking you somewhere else—what's in store for you there is probably worse than anything that might happen at the first location.

HOW TO FLY AN AMERICAN FLAG

35

Oh, say does that star-spangled banner yet wave over your front porch? If so, hopefully you already know all your Old Glory etiquette. But if you'd like to show some patriotic spirit and just aren't sure about all those flag-flying dos and don'ts, here are the rules:

1. Fly your flag from sunrise to sunset only, unless you have a light to illuminate the flag after dark.

2. If you want to display your flag in a window, hang it horizontally or vertically (using tacks, tape, whatever) with the stars in the upper left from the point of view of people on the street.

3. Carry and display the flag carefully so it never touches the ground. Contrary to what you might think, if you do accidentally drop it, you don't have to burn it, but you should pick it up and dust if off as quickly as possible.

4. If you have anything other than a nylon, all-weather flag (the most common kind), keep the flag inside in bad weather.

5. Fold the flag properly whenever you take it down. With another person's help, hold the flag waist-high and parallel to the ground, making sure you and your assistant hang on to all four corners rather than letting one edge drop. Now fold the flag in half lengthwise so the bottom striped half covers the stars, then fold it in half lengthwise again so half the stars fold over the stripes. Next, make a triangular fold by folding the exposed striped corner up so it meets the opposite edge of the flag. Fold the outer point in to make another triangular fold. Repeat these triangular folds until there's nothing left but a blue triangle of stars and a small section of fabric. Finish by tucking this section into the top fold of the triangle.

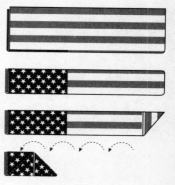

6. Store the folded flag on a shelf or anywhere it's protected and not touching the floor.

7. If your flag looks dirty, wash or dry-clean it. If it gets stained, frayed, or damaged, however, better call your local chapter of the Veterans of Foreign Wars (vfw.org), the American Legion (legion.org), or the Elks Lodge (elks.org). They'll take your flag and burn it in a dignified ceremony.

HOW TO USE CHOPSTICKS

36

Chopsticks may be the centuries-old utensils of choice for eating Asian cuisine, but there's no ancient Chinese secret to using them. All it takes is proper positioning and a little practice. Here's how:

1. If you're given chopsticks in a paper holder, take them out and pull them apart.

2. Using the hand you write with and pointing the narrower end of the chopstick down, place the wider end of one chopstick at the base of your thumb (between the thumb and index finger) and position the other end on the top of your ring finger. This will be your bottom chopstick.

3. With that same hand, hold the other chopstick with your index finger, middle finger, and thumb, just like you'd hold a pen. This will be your top chopstick.

4. To pick up food, bend your index and middle fingers to move the tip of the top chopstick closer to the bottom chopstick, then grab a piece of food between them. Always keep the bottom chopstick stationary; the top is the only one that should move.

5. If they're provided, use spoons or serving chopsticks (not your own) to serve yourself. If not, use the clean top ends of your chopsticks when taking food from a communal dish.

6. If you're faced with a big morsel that won't fit in your mouth as is, pick it up with your chopsticks and bite off a piece. Don't spear food with your chopsticks.

7. Assuming there's no chopstick rest available, place your chopsticks across the top of your dish when not in use. Never stick your chopsticks into your rice and leave them there—it's considered extremely rude.

HOW TO LOOK GREAT IN PHOTOS

37

Are you ready for your close-up? Looking good for life's many Kodak moments doesn't require graduating from John Casablancas or being surrounded 24/7 by your very own coterie of makeup artists and fashion stylists. Here's how to be pretty as a picture and start filling your album with flattering photos:

1. Avoid bold prints; you don't want to be overwhelmed by your outfit. And if you're light-skinned, steer clear of bright white clothing around your face—it'll make you look washed out.

2. Apply foundation and a little concealer under your eyes to help smooth out skin tone and eliminate shadows. Then dust on powder, concentrating on your forehead, nose, and chin so your face won't look shiny. Apply the rest of your makeup with a slightly heavier hand than usual, but be careful not to overemphasize any one feature. In other words, forget the smoky eyes and nude lips: no matter how

good it looks off camera, it won't translate well on film.

3. Soft, late-afternoon sun is the most flattering for photos. Avoid direct overhead light, whether indoor or outdoor. If you're being photographed outside at high noon, head for the shade, but be sure it's an even shade; dappled light creates weird shadow effects.

4. If you're getting snapped standing, transfer your weight to your back foot. If you're sitting, slide forward slightly, keeping your knees together and to one side so they're not photographed straight on.

5. Position yourself at a forty-five-degree angle to the camera. Don't press your arms against your sides; instead, keep them slightly away from your body to make them look svelter.

6. For the most flattering face shot, bring your chin forward, tilt your head down, and look up slightly.

7. Act natural. Remember, if you feel awkward, you'll probably look awkward. And skip saying "cheese"—

it's a great way to end up getting caught with your mouth half open.

8. Smile! If you're feeling tense, take a breath, look away, and then look back at the camera.

HOW TO MAKE A TOAST

If you want to be the toastess with the mostest, skip the speeches and the blow-by-blows of your lifelong buddyship with the toastee. Whether you're thanking your host for gathering friends for Sunday brunch or paying tribute to your little brother and his bride on their wedding day, keep it brief. Remember, your goal is simply to honor whoever you're toasting and charm your audience. Here's how to do just that:

1. Be prepared. Think about what the person being toasted means to you and who your audience will be. Write out what you want to say and practice until you've got it down. Never give a toast using notes. If you're asked to make an impromptu toast, take a moment to collect your thoughts and then say a few words about why the person you're toasting is special to you.

2. Time your toast properly. Wait until everyone's been served a drink, and never make a toast until after

the host has had the chance to do so. However, if you're halfway through dessert and it's clear that the host isn't planning to propose any toasts, go right ahead.

3. Pick up your glass, and unless you're with a small, informal group, stand up.

4. Say, "Could I please have everyone's attention? I'd like to propose a toast." Although you may have seen others tap their glasses with a utensil to signal a toast, it's better to simply speak up and announce it than risk fine crystal.

5. Be flattering and appropriate. Remember, it's a toast, not a roast. Funny anecdotes are great, but forget the inside jokes and really embarrassing stories and stick with something everyone can enjoy.

6. Make it short and simple—no more than three minutes or the crowd could get restless. Something as brief as a few sentences is perfectly acceptable.

7. Be yourself. If you're naturally witty, wonderful, but don't sweat it if you're not a stand-up comic. Just be sincere and express your admiration for the toastee.

8. Keep the tone conversational so you'll sound natural. And no matter how many butterflies you have in your stomach, never say anything like "I'm a little nervous" or "Bear with me."

9. Speak loudly, especially if it's a large crowd.

10. Finish by inviting everyone to raise a glass toward the toastee, then take a sip of your drink. Cheers!

HOW TO WEAR RED LIPSTICK

39

Want to look sexier in thirty seconds flat? Slick on a coat of red lipstick and become the major minx you deep-down already are. Look, nothing gets attention like daring, powerful, classic red. If you've always secretly wanted to wear it, but weren't sure if you could—well, you certainly can. Here's how:

1. Choose the right shade for your skin tone. If you've got warm skin (meaning it has golden undertones), go for an orangey or brownish red. If your skin tone is cool (skin with pink or bluish undertones), pick a pinkish or purplish red.

2. Get a lip pencil in a similar shade to your lipstick and use it to fill in both your lips completely, giving your lipstick extra staying power. Don't color outside the natural line of your mouth when applying—trying to make your lips look fuller just ends up looking fake.

3. Carefully put on your lipstick. Red doesn't forgive mistakes easily, so if you veer outside the natural line of your mouth, it may be difficult to completely get off. If you have a lip brush, use it; it'll allow you to apply color more precisely.

4. Separate a tissue into two layers, and use one to blot your lips and remove excess lipstick.

5. Still holding the tissue to your lips, brush loose face powder over it. A fine dusting will go through the tissue and set your color.

6. To prevent your eyes from competing with your lips for attention, keep your eye makeup neutral.

7. Take your lip pencil, lipstick, and powder with you for touch-ups out on the town. No matter what cosmetics companies would have you believe, there is no lipstick in existence that doesn't eventually come off with eating, drinking, or smooching. Speaking of which, red is a great color to wear for cocktails, but you might want to substitute another shade if you're on your way to dinner: eating an entire meal will rub off most of the red, leaving a line around your lips that'll be much more noticeable than something more neutral.

HOW NOT TO GET RIPPED OFF
BY A MECHANIC

Getting your car repaired is no Sunday drive in the country, but if you know what you're doing, you'll majorly minimize both your cash outflow and Advil intake. Here's how to locate a good shop and make sure you get the best service:

1. As soon as you buy your car, get recommendations for mechanics (or service technicians, as they're sometimes called) from friends, family, and coworkers—especially those with the same kind of car as yours. Ideally, you'll have a few places in mind before you really need them rather than being forced to make a rush decision. Keep in mind that if something goes wrong with your car while it's still under warranty, you'll need to go to the dealership to have the repair covered. However, if your car simply needs servicing such as an oil change, don't assume you have to go to the dealer until your warranty expires; any independent licensed mechanic should be able to do the work without affecting the warranty. If your warranty is no longer

valid or you're getting work done that's not covered under it, you may want to go to a smaller shop rather than the dealer, since independent mechanics often offer more personal service and charge less.

2. Find a neat and orderly shop with modern-looking equipment. If there are cars worth roughly the same amount as yours in the parking lot, that's another good sign.

3. Ask if the shop frequently does repair work on the type of car you've got. The staff should be courteous and willing to answer your questions.

4. Look for certificates on the walls indicating that the shop has been approved by the American Automobile Association (AAA) and that its technicians have been certified by the National Institute for Automotive Service Excellence (ASE). Community or customer service awards are another plus.

5. Find out about labor costs (do they charge by the hour, a flat rate, or what?), diagnostic fees, guarantees, and acceptable forms of payment. You might want to consider only going to a place that

takes credit cards; that way, if you have a dispute with the shop, your credit card company may be able to withhold payment until the situation is investigated.

6. Start going to one shop for regular maintenance jobs so you can build a relationship with your mechanic before there's a problem.

7. As soon as something does go wrong, check your owner's manual. If you can't fix it yourself, you may at least get a better idea of what the problem is.

8. When you bring your car in for a repair, describe the symptoms to the technician (or the service writer, if it's a large shop), but don't try to get him to diagnose it right away or tell him how you think he should fix it. At the same time, don't admit you're clueless either, even if that's how you feel.

9. Ask to be notified once the problem has been identified and the cost of repairs determined. If you need expensive or complicated repairs, or if you have any doubts about the recommended work, get a second opinion.

10. Before you give the go-ahead on any work, get a signed, written estimate describing the repairs to be done, the parts required, and the expected labor costs. The estimate should also say that the shop will get your approval before doing any work beyond the agreed-upon time and cost.

11. When the work is finished, get a receipt detailing what's been done (which you should keep for your records), ask for all replaced parts, and test-drive your car to be sure you're satisfied with the repairs. If there's a problem, it's better to address it immediately.

12. If you do have a dispute regarding billing or the quality of the work, talk to the technician first. Be friendly and polite. Can't resolve the problem? Discuss it with the shop's manager or owner. If that doesn't work, contact your local consumer protection agency or the AAA or ASE (assuming the shop is accredited by them). And if all else fails, you can always file a claim in small claims court.

WHAT TO DO IF SOMEONE FAINTS

41

You're hiking up Pike's Peak when your pal, spotting a snake, passes out. What now? Fainting may be no big deal—it can occur in otherwise healthy people due to causes such as anxiety, fear, pain, hunger, or overheating—but it can also be caused by a serious condition, such as heart disease or epilepsy. That's why it should be treated as a medical emergency until the fainter comes to and you have a better idea of the cause. Till then, here's what to do:

1. If the fainter is sitting, carefully put his head between his knees. If he's lying down, raise his legs above heart level using pillows, books, or whatever's handy.

2. Watch the fainter's mouth—fainting victims sometimes vomit and then choke. Gently turn his head to the side so his tongue doesn't block his breathing and he won't choke if he vomits. If he does start to throw up, turn him on his side and use your fingers to sweep out his mouth afterward.

3. If the fainter isn't breathing, call 911. If you're trained in CPR, start performing it; if not and there are others nearby, yell, "Does anyone know CPR?" If the fainter *is* breathing, get blood flow going to the brain by raising his legs above his head. Loosen any tight clothes, especially at the neck and waist, and if you have one around, put a washcloth dampened with cool water on his face. If, however, he feels cold, cover him with a blanket. He should regain consciousness within a minute or two; if not, call 911.

4. Once the fainter comes to, don't let him get up immediately. If he's been sitting, raise his feet for a few minutes before he stands up. If he's lying down, have him stay in that position for a few minutes, then make him sit up for several more minutes before letting him stand. When he does get up, stand close by so you can catch him if he faints again.

HOW TO RESCUE A BABY BIRD
THAT'S FALLEN FROM ITS NEST

42

Seeing a helpless little birdie on the ground can bring out the Florence Nightingale in any friend of a feather. But unless you know for sure that the cardinal in question is injured or its parents are dead, watch from afar for a while before you turn your home into an orphanage for ailing bird babies. If the wee chirper still looks like it's in dire distress, there's no need to wing it—here's what to do:

1. If you find a baby bird that's featherless or partially feathered (also known as a nestling), pick it up and put it back in its nest. Despite what you might've heard, its parents won't reject it if it's been touched by humans—as it happens, birds actually have a really poor sense of smell. However, you should put on gloves beforehand or pick it up with a towel, since birds can carry diseases. Watch from a distance over the next few hours to make sure its parents return to the nest. If they don't, call your local humane society or National Audubon Society chapter so they can put you in touch with a wildlife

rehabilitator who's trained to handle this sort of thing.

2. If you can't find the bird's nest or it's been destroyed, make a new one: first, punch several drainage holes in the bottom of a plastic margarine tub or small box, then line it with dry grass or leaves. If you know where the old nest was, place your new one near it in the same tree; if not, put your nest in the tree closest to where you found the nestling. Thread twine through a few of the holes in the bottom and tie it securely to the branch, then watch for the parents to come back and care for the bird. If they don't, ring the humane society or Audubon chapter for a referral to a wildlife rehabilitator who can take over.

3. If you find a young feathered bird hopping around (also known as a fledgling), don't automatically assume it's injured or abandoned. Chances are, it's hopping simply because it's still learning to fly. Never put a fledgling back in its nest—it could jump out and get hurt in the fall. Instead, shoo it to a more protected area of bushes or tall grass, and try to keep dogs and cats away from the area. Move well out of sight and watch for the parents to return.

If they don't? You guessed it—time to bring in the wildlife rehabilitator.

4. If you find a nestling or fledgling that's clearly injured or whose parents you know have been killed, call a wildlife rehabilitator. In the meantime, keep the bird safe in a dark, covered shoebox with air holes in the lid and with a heating pad set on low (or a rubber glove filled with hot water) under one half of the box. Don't feed or handle the bird, and definitely don't get any ideas about nursing the bird back to health yourself or keeping it as a pet—that's illegal. Wait for the wildlife rehabilitator to treat it.

HOW TO SLEEP WITH A SNORER

 -

If you dread going to bed, it's time to stifle your sweetie's snoring once and for all—no smothering with a pillow necessary! After all, sawing wood, best left to lumberjacks, definitely doesn't belong in the boudoir. Here's how to keep him from keeping you up:

1. Flabby throat tissues are a major cause of obstructed breathing and snoring, so encourage your mate to eat right and exercise by doing it yourself. If you lead by example, he'll be more likely to stay on course.

2. If you smoke, stop—at least around him. Secondary smoke can lead to nasal and lung congestion, a major cause of snoring. It also may encourage him to light up, which adds up to even more severe congestion.

3. Skip the midnight munchies and nightcaps with your man. Food and alcohol just before bedtime can cause muscles to slacken, potentially obstructing air

passages between the nose and lungs and resulting in—surprise!—snoring.

4. Don't give him sleeping pills or other sedatives, since they relax neck muscles and throat tissues and make snoring worse.

5. Dust and vacuum often to reduce bedroom allergens (such as pet dander, dust, and mold) and alleviate nasal stuffiness. Allergies limit airflow through the nose, forcing him to breathe through his mouth, where more flabby tissues are located.

6. Sew a pocket into the back of his pajama top and stick a tennis ball in it. This will make lying on his back pretty uncomfortable and get him to roll over onto his side—without your having to kick him first. Lying on his back lets his tongue fall backward into his throat, narrowing his airway and partially obstructing airflow.

7. Take the pillows off the bed. They can put a kink in his neck, contributing to airway obstruction.

8. Encourage him to try to go to sleep and get up at about the same time every day and avoid getting overtired.

9. If none of the above works, suggest he see a doctor, who may recommend dental devices, nasal strips, or surgery. And if his snoring is very loud or interrupted by periods of no breathing at all, or he often feels extreme fatigue or daytime sleepiness, make a doctor's appointment for him pronto—in some cases, snoring can indicate a serious medical condition such as obstructive sleep apnea.

10. Get yourself some earplugs or a white-noise CD so you can get some rest.

HOW TO SHUCK AN OYSTER

44

Next time you invite Dreamboat to dinner, serve that classic aphrodisiac: oysters on the half-shell. Since they're eaten raw, preparing them is a cinch—all you have to know is how to open the shell. Two tips before you buy: look for oysters tagged with the name of the place they're from; eating oysters from anywhere other than licensed, regularly inspected areas can lead to an ardor-abating bout of food poisoning. And only purchase oysters with a mild, sweet smell and tightly closed shells—that's what tells you they're still alive and fresh. Now, to shuck those shells:

1. Scrub oyster shells with a hard bristle brush under cold, running water and rinse thoroughly.

2. Put on a pair of sturdy kitchen gloves and grab an oyster so the cupped side's facing down. Hold it in a dish towel over a bowl.

3. Insert a knife (preferably an oyster knife, but any knife with a short, thick blade and strong handle

will do) into the hinge between the shells at the pointed end of the oyster. Twist the knife to separate the shells and then cut through the hinge muscle. Catch any liquid (known as the oyster liquor) in the bowl and set it aside.

4. Use the knife to scrape the meat from its shell, but don't remove it.

5. Get out a platter and cover it with crushed ice or small cubes. Then arrange the shells on the ice, both to keep them chilled and so they don't tip over.

6. Pour the oyster liquor over the oysters.

7. Slurp the raw meat straight from the half-shell or add lemon juice, cocktail sauce, or horseradish. If it's a more formal occasion, remove the meat from the shell with a small fork and dip it in sauce.

All right, so maybe you can't challenge a two-hundred-pound guy to an arm-wrestling match and expect to emerge victorious. But since size doesn't matter when it comes to darts, there's no reason not to throw down next time you're feeling competitive during a pub crawl. Ready, aim, fire away:

1. Learn the basics about the board. It's divided into pie-slice sections numbered 1 through 20, with the numbers indicating the point value you receive if your dart lands in that section. At the center of the board are two circles, known as the bull. The outer circle of the bull is worth twenty-five points, while the inner circle, known as the bull's-eye, is worth double that (fifty points). There are also two thin rings on the board; the inner ring counts for triple the number that section's worth, and the outer ring counts for double.

2. Challenge someone to a game of 301, one of the most popular dart games. The basic idea: Each

player starts with 301 points and tries to get down
to zero with as few darts as possible.

3. Take your place at the throwing line. You're about to
figure out who goes first by taking turns throwing a
dart at the center of the board; whoever comes
closest to the bull's-eye gets to start the game.

4. Stand just behind the throwing line with your feet
flat and slightly apart. Position yourself in the
stance that feels most comfortable and balanced—
either both feet facing forward or one foot forward
and the foot opposite your throwing hand pointed
out at a forty-five-degree angle.

5. Grip the center
of the dart firmly
between the
thumb and
fingertips of your
throwing hand.
You can use your
thumb and one to
four fingers to
grip the dart—do
whatever feels
most natural.

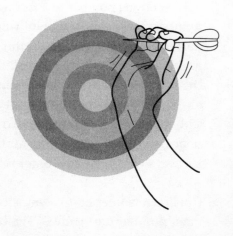

6. Hold the dart slightly in front of you and aim it at your target.

7. Bring the dart toward your cheek, relaxing your wrist back while keeping the dart parallel to the floor. Then throw the dart straight toward the board using your wrist and elbow rather than your shoulder. The dart should move quickly and smoothly, not wobble, and your thumb and fingers should be pointing toward your target as you release the dart.

8. Follow through on your throw. Once you've launched the dart, your forearm should be extended toward the board at about a forty-five-degree angle, with your thumb and fingers still pointing at it.

9. Check where your dart landed in relation to the other players'. If yours is closest to the bull's-eye, you go first; if it's second-closest, you go second; etc.

10. As soon as it's your turn, aim for the double-value outer ring or the bull's-eye, because in order to start reducing your score from 301, you have to first get your dart in one of those two areas (also known as hitting a double). You get three chances,

since each player throws three darts per turn. Once you hit a double, that dart and all others count toward your score. By the way, all dart throws count, but darts that miss the board, fall off, or stick into another dart don't get any score.

11. To win, you must be the first person to knock your score to zero by hitting a double. For example, if you have thirty-two points left to get to zero, you'd try to hit double sixteen, but if you rack up more points than you need, your score reverts back to what it was before that throw. For example, if you need double sixteen, but score double nineteen (or thirty-eight points) instead, your score stays at thirty-two.

WHAT TO DO IF YOUR CAR
BREAKS DOWN AT NIGHT

46

The chances of your car conking out on a lonely highway traveled solely by serial killers after sunset can be significantly reduced by taking your vehicle in for regular tune-ups and making sure you've got plenty of gas to get where you're going. It's also smart to avoid desolate stretches of road, carry a cell phone, and let others know your travel plans. But since being prepared can't prevent every problem, here's what to do in case your car does break down after dark:

1. At the first sign of car trouble, carefully get your car over to the right shoulder of the road, being extremely alert to other traffic. To ensure other cars will see you, avoid stopping just over the crest of a hill or on a curve. If you're on a highway, try to reach an exit before pulling over.

2. Once you've pulled well off the road, make your vehicle visible to other drivers. Turn on your hazard lights, lift the hood, and, if you have them, put reflector triangles or safety flares well behind your

car. (It's smart to keep a set of reflectors or flares along with a flashlight, tool kit, first-aid supplies, and a blanket and heavy jacket in your trunk at all times for emergencies like this.)

3. If you're a member of an automobile club, use your cell phone to call them for help. If not, call a relative or friend and ask them to look up the number of a 24-hour towing service, or, if you're out of town, call 911—the dispatcher will connect you to the local police, who can send an officer to escort you to a safer location and/or give you the number for a tow truck. If you don't have a phone, keep in mind that many major highways have call boxes along the right shoulder so you can contact the police in an emergency. If you see one nearby, walk to it, using extreme caution to stay off the road and out of the way of oncoming cars. If there's no call box or phone service available, wait in your car until someone stops to help, then open your window slightly and ask them to call the police. Remember, you don't know who this person is, so don't get out of your car.

4. After requesting assistance, wait inside your locked car (assuming it's safely out of the way of traffic). And keep your seatbelt on—remember, you could

still be hit from behind. If someone stops, just open your window a crack and let him know that you appreciate his concern, but help's already on the way.

HOW TO PREVENT JET LAG

47

You may not be able to avoid lost luggage or bad airplane food, but at least you can make sure jet lag doesn't accompany you on your next trip. Long-distance air travel across time zones confuses your internal body clock and can cause fatigue, irritability, poor concentration, disorientation, and sleep problems. Here's how to leave jet lag behind:

1. Get plenty of rest before you travel, and start adjusting your sleep patterns to be more in sync with your destination time zone several days before your trip; even a change of one or two hours helps.

2. Eat several small, light meals on the days before, during, and just following your flight, since big, heavy portions may make you feel sluggish. You should also steer clear of sugary snacks and caffeine, which can leave you jittery and inhibit your ability to sleep.

3. Once you're on your flight, reset your watch and try to match your sleep and meal schedule with whatever it'll be where you're headed. If it's nighttime at your destination, try to snooze on the plane; if it's daytime, try to stay awake, no matter what time your body thinks it is.

4. Drink lots of water on the plane. Since cabin air is extremely dry, it's easy to become dehydrated, which worsens the symptoms of jet lag.

5. Avoid alcohol while airborne. The impact of booze on the body can be more than twice as potent at high altitudes, affecting sleep quality and causing dehydration. And needless to say, arriving at your destination with a hangover can keep you from feeling your freshest.

6. Exercise. Okay, you can't do calisthenics on the plane, but try to move around, walk up and down the aisle, and stretch in order to combat cramping, stiffness, and swelling in your legs and feet.

7. Pace yourself on arrival. If possible, arrange your schedule so you don't have to rush into an important meeting or head off on a long sightseeing bus tour.

Chill out for a little while and try to go to sleep at your usual hour in the new time zone.

8. Soak up the sun. Sunlight helps reset your internal clock, so spend some time outside during the first few days at your destination.

48

Next time your fellow's fixing to tie one on, sidle up to him and offer an assist. (Later, if you like, you can take the tie off and put it to more creative use.) In the meantime, here's your guide to getting your guy necktied:

1. Stand by your man (well, okay, in front of him) and turn his collar up.

2. Put the tie around his neck, front side up, with the wide end on your left and extending about a foot lower than the narrow end.

3. Cross the wide end over the narrow end about an inch down from the collar.

4. Cross the wide end back under the narrow end (again about an inch down from the collar).

5. Cross the wide end over the narrow end again (yep, one inch down).

6. Pull the wide end behind the knot, then up and through the loop at the neck.

7. Pull the wide end down and through the front of the knot, holding it loose with your index finger.

8. Pull down on the wide end while using your other hand to push up and tighten the knot.

9. Pull down on the narrow end while sliding the knot all the way up to the collar. If you've done it right, the tip of the wide end should touch his belt buckle.

10. Lift the wide end of the tie and tuck the narrow end through the tie tag on the back, then neaten the knot and turn down the collar.

HOW TO GET RED WINE OUT OF A RUG

49

Everyone knows it's not a real party till someone spills a carafe of Chianti on the carpet. Just don't wait until morning to clean it up—the faster you move, the more likely your shag can be saved. Okay, ideally, you should read and follow the care instructions and warnings provided by your carpet's manufacturer, especially if your rug is made with natural fibers. However, there are a few basic steps that will work with most carpets:

1. Blot the stain with paper towels to remove as much of it as possible.

2. Mix one part white vinegar with one part lukewarm water, then pour a little on the stain. (If you don't have white vinegar on hand, you can also use club soda or white wine straight out of the bottle.)

3. Blot with paper towels.

4. Mix a half-teaspoon of mild dishwashing liquid (one that contains no bleach, such as Dawn) with a cup of lukewarm water. Soak a paper towel in this mixture, then wring it out and dab the spot with it. Blot.

5. Repeat until the stain is removed.

6. Soak another paper towel in lukewarm tap water, then wring it out and dab the spot with it.

7. Blot with paper towels to remove excess moisture.

HOW TO GRILL A BURGER

50

Come on, baby, light your fire! No need for a guy or a super-deluxe backyard barbecue system big enough to cook up an entire cattle herd. Armed with a cheap, portable grill, you'll be flipping burgers in no time. Now get cooking:

1. Get a bag of "self-lighting" charcoal briquettes at a grocery or hardware store. This is the simplest type—no lighter fluid required. How much charcoal will you need? It takes about thirty briquettes (a little less than half a five-pound bag) to grill one pound of meat. Weather conditions should also be factored in; if it's really windy, cold, or humid, you'll need to add more briquettes to build a good fire.

2. Set up your grill in a safe, open area on level ground, and keep it away from kids, pets, fences, overhanging branches, and bushes.

3. Remove the cooking rack from the grill and apply vegetable oil with a paper towel or spray on non-

stick cooking spray to prevent burgers from sticking to the rack once you start cooking.

4. Stack the briquettes in a pyramid formation in the center of the grill and light them with a match.

5. After lighting the briquettes, let them burn for at least fifteen minutes or whatever time is recommended on the package. They'll be ready for grilling when they're covered in light gray ash. (Black coals are too cool for cooking, bright red coals are too hot, and a mixture of red and black coals produces an uneven heat.)

6. For four burgers, mix a pound of ground chuck with a half-teaspoon of salt and a quarter-teaspoon of pepper. Divide the meat into four patties, making each one about an inch thick. Wearing an oven mitt, use a metal spatula or other long-handled tool to spread the coals evenly across the bottom of the grill or coal grate into an area about an inch or two larger than the area on the cooking rack that'll be covered by the burgers.

7. Check the temperature of the coals by carefully putting your palm a few inches above the cooking rack and then counting the seconds (one one

thousand, two one thousand . . .) until you need to move your hand away. Two seconds means the temperature is hot, four seconds is medium, and five seconds is low.

8. Cook ground-beef patties over medium heat for five or six minutes on each side for medium-done burgers and seven or eight minutes on each side for well-done. Try to keep the heat as even as possible while you grill. If the fire's too cool, the burgers won't sizzle, and if the fire's too hot, the outside of the burgers will cook quickly, but the insides will remain uncooked. To increase the heat, rake the coals closer together and knock off some ash, lower the cooking rack, or open the grill's vents. To decrease heat, do the opposite.

9. If you want to serve the burgers on a platter, get a new one from the kitchen. Never serve cooked burgers on the same unwashed plate you used to carry raw meat to the grill, since it could harbor harmful bacteria.

10. Once you've finished grilling, but while the cooking rack is still warm, scrub it with a wadded-up piece of aluminum foil. Then remove the rack and wash it with mild detergent and water, rinsing well.

11. Cover the grill (if there is a cover), close its vents and let the coals burn out completely and the ashes cool for forty-eight hours.

12. Scoop the ashes out with a trowel and throw them away.

HOW TO JUMP—START A CAR

51

If you don't own jumper cables, then hello, go get some before you need them. Hey, they're only twenty-five bucks, which will seem a small price to pay when you're stranded in a blizzard. Of course, if you don't have your own, you'll have to wait around for someone who does. What then? Read on:

1. Make sure the donor car runs on the same voltage as yours. Twelve-volt batteries are standard these days, but check the battery to be sure—it should say what voltage it is on top. If the batteries aren't compatible, thank the good Samaritan in the vintage Volvo and wait for another car to come along and help you.

2. Park the good car next to or facing—but not touching—the dead one, and make sure both cars are turned off and in park (or neutral if the car is a stick).

3. Open the hood and check out the battery of the dead car. If you see gunk around the terminals (those little

metal parts sticking up that look like bolts), wipe it off. See any cracks in the plastic casing? Forget it— you need a new battery. If you belong to an automobile association or have a warranty with roadside assistance, now would be a good time to call. Failing that, call a tow truck to take you directly to Sears or another nearby battery retailer. Don't mess with this—if you try to jump-start a cracked battery, it could blow up (yes, as in explode).

4. Each battery has two metal terminals, one marked positive (+) and one marked negative (−). Attach one end of the positive (red or orange) jumper cable to the positive terminal of the dead car's battery.

5. Attach the other end of the positive cable to the positive terminal of the good car's battery.

6. Attach one end of the negative (black) cable to the negative end of the good car's battery.

7. Attach the other end of the negative cable to the dead car's engine block (any solid metal part of the engine frame), away from the battery. Although you may be tempted, based on the logical pattern you've discerned thus far, don't attach it to that car's negative terminal! Again, you risk battery explosion.

8. Get whoever's helping you to start their car and give it a little gas while still in park.

9. Wait a minute, then try to start your car. With luck it'll start pretty easily. If so, let both cars idle for a couple of minutes. If not, wait a few seconds and try again. If it doesn't start after a few tries, your battery is permanently dead, friend. To review: call your automobile association or roadside assistance program if you have one; if not, better get a tow truck.

10. Now, disconnect the cables in reverse order from the way you attached them. That is, start by disconnecting the engine block and end by disconnecting the positive terminal of the car you just restarted.

11. Thank your rescuers profusely. You may even want to offer them twenty bucks for the trouble.

12. Go on your merry little way. If you can, drive the car for at least a half-hour to ensure it recharges properly; otherwise, you might need another jump next time you start the car.

HOW TO FIND A BRA THAT FITS

 -

You don't have to be Pamela Anderson to switch bra sizes. Breasts change over the years, so if you've been wearing the same size ever since you graduated out of training bras, it's time to once again test how your chest measures up.

1. Enlist a friend to measure you with a cloth or flexible plastic tape measure so you can stand in a relaxed, natural position and get the most accurate reading. Or visit a lingerie shop or intimate apparel department and ask an assistant to help you (in which case you won't need to bring a tape measure—they should have one on hand).

2. Wearing an unpadded, comfortable bra, measure around your rib cage directly under your breasts, holding the tape measure straight around your body. Add five to the number of inches you come up with. If your new number is odd, round up to the next even number, since bras generally

only come in even sizes. This number is your frame size.

3. Measure completely around the fullest part of your chest, holding the tape measure straight without pulling tight. The number you get is your bustline measurement.

4. Figure out your cup size by subtracting your frame size measurement (step #2) from your bustline measurement (step #3). Find the difference in the chart below:

0 to 1 inch	AA
1 to 2 inches	A
2 to 3 inches	B
3 to 4 inches	C
4 to 5 inches	D
5 to 6 inches	DD

This method should give you a pretty accurate measurement, but remember that you may wear a slightly different size depending on the brand of bra. Ultimately, go with whatever feels best. If the tape measure says you're a 34B, but a 34C looks and feels more comfortable, get the 34C.

5. To double-check that a bra fits you properly, ask yourself these questions: do the cups fit smoothly without gapping or squeezing? Does the place where the cups meet at the bottom lie almost flat against your breastbone? Is the bottom of the bra straight all around or even slightly lower in the back? Is the bottom band snug but not tight? If so, buy it!

HOW TO EAT A LOBSTER

53

You've seen people eat lobster. In fact, you've stared at them enviously while consuming yet another piece of hum-drum jumbo shrimp (yawn). You want a lobster bib of your own, but you're intimidated. And who wouldn't be, with those beady eyes looking up at you, watching to see if you're doing it right? Well, place that order, because here's what to do next:

1. Pick up the lobster with one hand and use your other hand to snap off the large claws at the front of the body.

2. Crack each claw with a nutcracker, pliers, or a heavy knife, then use a pick or lobster fork to remove the meat. Dip it in melted butter if you like and pop it in your mouth.

3. Twist off the tail (which contains the most meat) and pull it away from the body. Force the meat out

in one piece using a fork or your thumb. Cut up the meat, dip, and eat.

4. Separate the top shell of the body from the bottom of the body, revealing a yellowish-greenish substance called the tomalley (liver). If it's a female lobster, you might also find reddish eggs (also known as coral or roe). Scrape this stuff out with a spoon and set aside to dip in butter and eat later if you're up for it.

5. Break apart the body. Use a lobster fork to separate the meat from the cartilage and eat.

6. Twist off the legs and snap them apart before sucking out the meat.

HOW TO IMPROVE YOUR CREDIT RATING

54

Ignorance may be bliss, but not when you're looking for a loan, job, or apartment. In those cases, it pays to know just how much of a financial risk you're perceived to be and then prepare to make that perceived risk as puny as possible. Here's how:

1. Get a copy of your credit report. Think of this report as a snapshot of how good you are (or aren't) with money. Fortunately, it's not a complete exposé that details how much you've spent on manicures or your shoe obsession, but it does list all the credit accounts you've had in the past ten years—credit cards, bank loans, mortgages—as well as amounts borrowed and owed, when accounts were opened and closed, and timeliness of payments. And anyone who wants to know how financially trustworthy you are (such as landlords, potential creditors, and employers) can buy a copy. But you can get one too, simply by requesting it from one of the three major credit bureaus:

- Equifax, at 800–997–2493 or equifax.com
- Experian, at 888–397–3742 or experian.com
- Trans Union, at 800–888–4213 or transunion.com

If you've recently been turned down for credit, the report will be free; otherwise, it'll cost you about eight to fifteen dollars.

2. Once you receive the report, read it carefully, since a full quarter of all credit reports contain at least one error. If you do find a mistake, contact the creditor directly and request that action be taken to correct the situation.

3. If your request to fix something in your report is declined or you feel the need to explain something— like why, for a specific period, you had financial issues—write a brief description (up to a hundred words) of everything negative you can account for. Then call each of the credit bureaus above and ask them to add it to your report. Be aware that, unlike other information in your report, this written statement won't automatically disappear after seven to ten years, so be sure to request that it be removed as soon as the period you're explaining no longer appears on your report. Otherwise, your statement could work against you, since creditors

might not know about an outdated problem without it.

4. Meanwhile, pay at least the minimum amount due on each credit card or loan every month to develop a history of responsible bill-paying. You don't want to further damage your credit by missing or being late with payments on an account, carrying high balances, or overextending yourself financially. If you're frustrated by a few missed payments from four years back or a check you bounced in college, recent positive marks can lessen the effect of earlier negative ones.

5. Beware of companies (the kind that often advertise on late-night TV) claiming to offer quick fixes for bad credit ratings. There are no magic-bullet solutions to repair a damaged credit rating, and these companies can't do anything for you that you can't do yourself. If you've got serious financial woes, contact a credit counseling agency who can help you consolidate and repay your debt. How it works: The agency negotiates with your credit card companies to reduce your interest rates and late fees. You then make single monthly payments to the agency, which in turn pays off each of your creditors. Some agencies offer their services for

free; others charge a nominal fee, usually between five and twenty-five dollars a month. In addition to helping you get out of debt and restore your credit rating, agency counselors also teach you money management skills so you can avoid future financial problems. Be sure to work with an accredited counselor; to find one in your area, contact the National Foundation for Credit Counseling at 800–388-2227 or nfcc.org.

HOW TO MIX A MARTINI

55

Go ahead, down your daiquiris, gulp your greyhounds, sip your Singapore slings. Drink fads come and go, but shaken or stirred, the martini retains its title as the king of cocktails. Here's the classic recipe:

1. Keeping in mind that a shot glass, also known as a jigger, holds one and a half ounces and a tablespoon holds half an ounce, combine two ounces of gin and one-half ounce dry vermouth (an aperitif wine flavored with herbs, in case you were wondering) in a cocktail shaker or mixing glass half full of ice. If you like your martini on the dry side, use less vermouth. By the way, yes, some people prefer their martinis made with vodka, but ignore them: the classic is always made with gin.

2. Shake or stir, then strain into a cocktail glass. Which makes a better martini? Some claim the drink should be shaken to properly combine the flavors; others prefer stirring so the gin doesn't get "bruised"

(a fancy word for cloudy), though it doesn't affect the way the drink tastes. Try both methods and decide for yourself—but either way, don't overmix.

3. Throw in a green olive, and if you want to make a "dirty" martini, add a little olive juice. If you prefer a twist to an olive, slice both ends off a lemon and make a lengthwise slit in the peel, then use your thumb and fingers to pull the peel away from the fruit. Next, cut the peel lengthwise into strips a quarter-inch wide. Twist one of these pieces (gently, or it'll break) over your glass to release its oils, then drop it into your drink.

HOW TO SELL YOUR CAR

56

If you're a wheeler-dealer who loves driving a hard bargain, steer clear of dealer trade-in offers and put your vehicle up for sale yourself. As long as you're not in a huge hurry to sell your old car, and you're patient enough to handle phone inquiries and test drives, prepared to get minor repairs done, and pretty shrewd in the negotiation department, eliminate the dealer middleman and you'll pull in the profit. Here's how:

1. Figure out how much to ask for. To help appraise the value of your vehicle, use the tools on automotive Web sites such as Edmunds.com and Kelley Blue Book (kbb.com) and check out local newspaper ads to find out what cars similar to yours are selling for. You can also look at car ads online at such sites as AutoTrader.com, Carpoint.com, and Cars.com. Then set your asking price at least five to ten percent higher than the price you really want so you have room to negotiate with a buyer—and still get what you want for the car.

2. If your car's not paid off, talk to the lender about how the loan will be paid and how the title should be transferred to the person who buys your car.

3. Wash and wax the exterior of the car and thoroughly clean the interior. Now would also be a good time to take down those fuzzy dice dangling from the rearview mirror and remove any other personal items—after all, you want prospective buyers to be able to picture the car as their own.

4. Check with your state's department of motor vehicles about change of ownership requirements, license plate transfers, and what forms you'll need to fill out.

5. Get your previous maintenance records out. If you don't have all the paperwork, your repair shop may be able to give you copies.

6. If your car is still covered by a standard warranty, check it to see if you can transfer it to a new owner. A warranty is an additional selling point, so if it's still valid, you'll want to let potential buyers know.

7 Have your mechanic inspect the car and put together a report on its condition. If the report

recommends any repairs, decide whether or not they're worth making in order to sell the car. Think about any issues a buyer could raise and how you'd respond. For example, are you prepared to lower the price to cover any suggested fixes?

8. Write your ad, using online and local newspaper ads as a model. Your ad should give potential buyers basic details such as the make, model, year, and description of the car, any selling points such as low mileage or fuel efficiency, and your phone number. Also include the asking price to weed out callers who just want to know how much the car is.

9. Advertise your car in as many places as you can: for example, online and newspaper classifieds, bulletin boards at your office or a nearby college, and a "For Sale" sign in your car window. Again, include your asking price.

10. To be on the safe side, arrange to meet prospective buyers before dark in a public place (such as a shopping mall), let someone else know where you'll be, and bring a friend with you. Avoid anyone who seems difficult or sketchy on the phone.

11. Go along for the ride on test drives—that way, you can answer any questions and ensure your car doesn't disappear off into the sunset.

12. Have your inspection report and maintenance records handy to show potential buyers.

13. If a prospect wants to have the car checked out by an independent mechanic, accompany him to the repair shop.

14. Negotiate. Bargaining is part of the process, but you should be willing to walk away from an offer if it's too low. Have your pricing research on hand to show that your asking number is reasonable.

15. Once you've agreed on a price, ask the buyer for a cashier's check or cash as payment; that way, you don't have to stress about the possibility of a personal check bouncing.

16. Sign over the title once you've received full payment and take care of any paperwork required by the department of motor vehicles. If the title isn't transferred, you could be held legally liable if the buyer's involved in any accidents.

17. Type up a bill including the names, addresses, and phone numbers of you and the buyer; the car's make, model, year, Vehicle Identification Number (VIN), and mileage; the full sale price and method of payment; and a statement that says the car was sold in "as is" condition without any warranty (unless it's still covered) or return policy. Print out two copies, sign and date both, and have the buyer do the same. Keep one for your records and give the other one to the buyer.

18. Cancel the insurance on the car you just sold.

19. If you live in a state where your license plates belong to you rather than your car, remember to take the plates off before you hand over the keys to the new owner.

WHAT TO DO WITH AN ARTICHOKE

 -

There you are, strolling through the produce department, picking up peaches, when suddenly what should you spy but a big bin of artichokes. Sure, when you're out to eat, there's nothing you love more than a good artichoke heart on a pizza or salad, but chow down on a whole artichoke at home? What are you supposed to do with the thing? Bake it? Barbecue it? Serve it with whipped cream and jimmies? Well, not exactly:

1. Pick an artichoke that feels heavy for its size and has thick, tightly closed, leaves. If you're buying one in the fall, you may notice brown streaks on the leaves. Ignore them—they're fine.

2. Turn the artichoke on its side and use a sharp serrated knife to cut the stem off so the artichoke will sit upright on a plate.

3. Cut off the top quarter of the artichoke.

4. If the tops of the outside layer of leaves feel thorny, use scissors to snip them off.

5. Rinse the artichoke so you get all the dirt out from between the leaves.

6. Pull off any loose leaves from around the bottom.

7. Rub the cut edges with a halved lemon so they don't get discolored.

8. To cook, fill a large pot with a couple inches of water, then add the juice of one lemon (about two tablespoons) and a tablespoon of salt.

9. Bring to a steady boil over high heat, covering the pot so the water will boil faster.

10. Wrap your hand in a dish towel to protect it from getting splashed by the boiling water, then put the artichoke right side up in the pot. Because the artichoke will float, the water won't cover it.

11. Return the water to a boil, then turn it down to medium-high heat and cook the artichoke

uncovered for twenty-five to forty minutes, depending on its size.

12. To test whether it's done, remove the artichoke from the pot with tongs or a slotted spoon and turn it upside down to quickly drain. Lay it on a plate and stick the tip of a knife into a center leaf. If it's ready, the leaf should pull out easily. If not, put it back in the pot, resume cooking, and test it again in five minutes.

13. When the artichoke is done, dump it into a colander in the sink and let it drain upside down.

14. As soon as the artichoke is cool enough to handle, put it on a plate.

15. To eat, start at the bottom and pull out a leaf with your fingertips.

16. If you want to dip the leaf in melted butter or vinaigrette, do it now.

17. Put the meaty end of the leaf in your mouth and scrape off the pulp with your teeth while pulling on the other end with your fingers.

18. Discard the leaf on your plate.

19. Work your way toward the middle of the artichoke, biting off the meaty end of the tender inner leaves rather than scraping them with your teeth. Pull out and discard the thin, immature leaves in the very center.

20. Use a spoon or small knife to scrape out the fuzzy inedible section now visible (called the choke). Avoid cutting into the artichoke heart beneath the choke—it's the meatiest, tastiest part.

21. When you get down to the heart, cut it into bite-size chunks, then dip the pieces or eat them plain.

HOW TO CHOOSE THE BEST GLASSES
FOR YOUR FACE

 -

If you think men don't make passes at girls who wear glasses, you're probably not wearing the right pair. Get framed by a set of specs that suit you and you'll not only see better, you'll look better too. Here's how to pick a pair with flair:

1. Wear your hair in your usual style and put on a favorite shirt in a neutral color.

2. Ask a friend to come with you to the eyewear shop to provide a second opinion. You may also want to bring a camera so you can get your pal or an employee to take photos of you in your favorite styles and decide which frames you like best at your leisure.

3. Look at your face in a mirror and determine if it's more angular or curved. Okay, you may be a combination of both, but decide which is dominant.

4. Choose a frame shape that contrasts with your face shape. If you've got an angular face, choose curved styles such as ovals or almonds that will soften the angles of your face. If you've got a curved face, choose rectangular frames; styles with crisp, straight lines will make your face look less round.

5. Match the top of the frames to your eyebrows—in other words, they should follow the same basic arc as the brows. If the frames sit beneath your brow, you'll look permanently surprised; if the frames are above your brows, on the other hand, it'll look like you're frowning or angry. That said, since small frames are currently in vogue, if you do choose a pair that falls below your brows, opt for a rimless or minimalist style that echoes your brows' natural curve.

6. When selecting a frame color, consider your skin tone. If you have skin with golden undertones, it's smart to opt for gold, brown, or another warm shade. If your skin has pinkish or bluish undertones, on the other hand, select silver, black, or another cool shade. Beyond that, go with whatever suits your personal taste.

7. Make sure the size and position of the frames' bridge (that tiny piece that sits on your nose and

holds the glasses together) helps balance your features. If you have close-set eyes, go with a lighter bridge and draw attention outward with color or trim at the temples. For wide-set eyes, draw attention inward toward the center of the face with a bridge that's dark, colored, or detailed. If you have a long nose, a straight, low bridge that's dark or colored will help visually break up the length of the nose. A bridge that sits high and turns up at the sides, however, will make your nose appear longer.

8. If you have questions or want help deciding, ask. Employees should be trained in helping customers pick out glasses that look good on them. If the staff doesn't seem helpful and knowledgeable, shop somewhere else.

9. If you brought a camera, have your friend or an employee take photos of you in the frames you like. That way, you can take a fresh look at them later and get other opinions before making a final decision.

WHAT TO DO WITH A HALF–FINISHED
BOTTLE OF WINE

59

Saturday's wine-tasting soiree was a smashing success, but what do you do with what didn't get drunk? Don't dump that leftover vino down the drain—store it right and you can sip it another evening instead. Here's how to keep opened wine tasting fine:

1. Stick the cork back in the bottle as soon as you finish pouring the wine. The idea is to limit its exposure to oxygen, the key culprit that makes its flavor change.

2. Put the bottle in the fridge—the lower temperature will keep the contents fresher longer and prevent bacteria from growing in the wine (yum!). White wines should last about two days, while reds might be good for three or four. If you don't get to it that quickly, however, you can always try it anyway. Recorked wine won't turn toxic; the worst that could happen is you'll take a sip of something that doesn't taste so great—the surest sign you should toss the wine.

3. If you want to save the vino for up to a week, get a can of inert gas such as Private Preserve Wine Preserver from a wine shop. Before refrigerating a half-finished bottle, you spray the gas into it, replacing most of the oxygen inside and slowing the wine's breakdown.

4. If it's a red you're storing, don't forget to take it out of the refrigerator an hour or two before you want to drink it to let it get closer to room temperature. If you pour it into glasses, it'll warm up a little faster.

5. When you're ready to reopen the wine, use a corkscrew rather than easing the cork out by hand. Refrigeration causes corks to dry out, so if you try to pull it out on your own, you could end up breaking it.

6. Don't want to *drink* the leftover wine? Use it for cooking. If you know you won't need it right away, you can even freeze the leftover wine in an ice-cube tray (a standard tray holds an eighth of a cup per cube). Once the cubes are frozen, transfer them to a plastic bag and take them out one at a time to use in recipes. But don't try to save old wine until it turns to vinegar; making proper vinegar from wine requires a starter and can take several months.

HOW TO GIVE A BACK MASSAGE

Motel bed magic fingers are fine, but if you really want to get your guy going, offer him a backrub from his own personal masseuse. Have him step into your massage parlor, light some scented candles, and prepare to make your man putty in your hands:

1. Pick a place to give the massage. A firm bed is good, but a soft one doesn't offer enough resistance; you don't want your subject to sink into the mattress every time you apply pressure. And forget the couch—there's not enough maneuvering room. If you don't have a firm bed, go with a carpeted floor.

2. Cover the surface with a large towel to protect it from massage oil spills. While you're at it, grab a hand towel and put it to the side so you can wipe off your hands and your guy's back after the massage. Warning: oil can stain towels, so don't use your favorite set for this.

3. Get out your massage oil. You can use stuff meant for massage, available in some bath specialty shops, or you can just use baby oil or even plain old corn or olive oil. Forget lotion: your hands will glide much better over oil, and you won't need to keep reapplying it.

4. Ask your subject to take off his shirt and lie down on his stomach.

5. Kneel down, straddle his butt, and sit on the top of his thighs.

6. Pour a little oil in your hands and rub them back and forth to warm it up. The oil will help your hands glide over his skin.

7. Starting at the top of the shoulders, use long, delicate, vertical strokes down to the lower back, then curve back up to the shoulders in one continuous movement. Repeat until the entire back, the tops of the shoulders, and the back of the neck are covered with a thin layer of oil. From now until the end of the massage, your hands should never leave your subject's skin—any break in contact would interrupt the relaxation you're working so hard to create.

8. Beginning at the lower back and moving up to the neck, put your thumbs flat on either side of your subject's spine and push out for about an inch, then bring the thumbs back to the starting position, only a little higher up. Never put direct pressure on the spine at any point in the massage; it can cause injury, and besides, it doesn't even feel good.

9. Sweep your hands down to the lower back using a long vertical stroke. Starting at the lower back, position your hands with the palms next to the spine and the fingers pointing outward. Using your palms, apply horizontal strokes till you reach the subject's sides, then sweep the palms back to the starting position, only a little higher up. Repeat until you get to the tops of the shoulders.

10. Knead the neck by grabbing onto a patch of flesh with one hand above the other, alternately squeezing it with first your left and then your right, moving your hands back and forth horizontally at the same time you move up and down the neck. Repeat on the tops of the shoulders, the back, and, if you're up for it, the butt. Keep in mind that you want to grab the flesh

so you get down to the muscle, not just pull on the skin.

11. Use your fingertips to feel around his shoulder blades for any tight, hard, knotty areas under the skin.

12. Apply pressure with the thumbs in circles over and around any knots.

13. Placing your fingers flat along either side of the spine, make small circles, starting at the lower back and moving up to the shoulders.

14. Using just your fingertips (not your nails), move up and down the back several times using vertical strokes, pressing down slightly and covering the entire back.

15. Repeat the last step, but this time apply almost no pressure at all. Your hands should feel like feathers on your subject's back.

16. Rest your hands on your subject's shoulders for a minute before removing them and ending the massage.

17. Thoroughly wipe off the massage oil from your hands with the hand towel, then use it to do the same thing to your guy's back. That way, the oil won't stain his clothes, sheets, etc.

HOW TO CUT A PINEAPPLE

 -

Can't swing tix to Hawaii? Sinking your teeth into a piece of fresh pineapple is the next best thing to doing the hula in Honolulu. A few things to know before you purchase your pineapple: it should smell sweet, its leaves should have little or no brown on the edges, and its shell should be green or gold with no mushy brown spots. Now, how to cut it:

1. Place the pineapple on its side and use a long, sharp knife to cut off the leafy crown, including the top part of the rind.

2. Slice off the bottom rind.

3. Stand the pineapple on its base and use wide, downward strokes to cut away the prickly exterior shell. Slice closely to save as much fruit as you can, but at the same time, make sure you go deep enough to cut away the eyes (those tough black dots under the skin). If you don't remove every bit of every eye, though, no big deal—they're edible.

4. Cut the pineapple in half lengthwise and then lengthwise again into quarters.

5. Remove the tough core by trimming about a quarter-inch from the center of each quarter.

6. Chop into bite-size pieces and chow down. Mmm, *ono!* (That's "delicious" in Hawaiian.)

7. Store leftover pineapple in an airtight container in the fridge and make sure you eat it within a few days.

HOW TO MAKE CUT FLOWERS LAST

 -

Do your daisies droop and your sunflowers slump too soon? If your bouquets stay for days, hooray! But if nay? Here's how to boost your flowers' power and lengthen their life:

1. When purchasing posies, always pick ones with firm, upright petals and buds that are just beginning to open. A list known for their longevity: anthurium, carnations, chrysanthemums, lilies, and orchids. With proper care, these flowers can often last as long as two weeks.

2. When you get your blooms home, hold stems under water, and cut one or two inches off the bottom at a forty-five-degree angle with a sharp knife or clippers. This prevents stems from sitting flat in the vase and creates a larger surface area, increasing their ability to suck up water.

3. Pull off any leaves that will fall below the water line of the vase. Leaves rot when submerged, causing algae and bacterial growth that can choke your flowers.

4. Fill a clean vase with water. If you got a packet of flower food from your florist, add that in as well.

5. Arrange your flowers in the vase, making sure all the stems are underwater.

6. Keep your bouquet away from direct sunlight, sources of heat like the tops of TVs and radiators, and drafts from air conditioners and fans.

7. Change the water daily. Yes, you'll lose any remaining benefits from the flower food, but fresh water keeps bacteria from growing in the vase, which is more important in the long run.

8. Recut the stems if they start to get soft and mushy. This gets rid of bacteria hampering the stems' ability to absorb water.

9. Once the flower show is over, clean the vase thoroughly to ensure your next bouquet lasts as

long as possible. If there's scum that doesn't want to come off or the vase's neck is too narrow for you to get your hand inside, buy a package of denture cleaner tablets at a drugstore, fill the vase with fresh water, add a tablet, and let sit for two hours before thoroughly rinsing out the vase.

HOW TO SIGNAL ON A BIKE

Until we all develop psychic powers, sharing the road means sharing your intentions. Using hand signals at least a hundred feet before your next move lets drivers and other bicyclists know what you're up to, making the streets safer for everybody. By the way, if you're driving and your turn signals or brake lights break, you can use these same signals. Here they are:

- *To turn left:* Extend your left arm and hand straight out.

- *To turn right:* Extend your left arm, bent at the elbow and facing up in an "L" shape. In some states, you can also signal a right turn by extending your right arm and hand straight out to the right side of your bike.

- *To slow down or stop:* Extend your left arm, bent at the elbow and facing down (an upside-down "L" shape).

HOW TO PLAY POKER

64 —

Sure, you gotta know when to hold 'em, know when to fold 'em, but first, you gotta spend some time perfecting your poker face in the mirror. Oh, and learn the basic rules of the game. Although there are many versions of poker, one of the simplest—and most popular—is five-card draw. Here's how you play:

1. Gather your players. Although you can play poker with just two people, five or six is ideal.

2. Decide on a betting limit and an ante with the other players. Although betting limits and antes aren't required, they're an especially good idea for beginners. A betting limit is simply the maximum amount players are allowed to put into the pot (the pile of money or poker chips in the middle of the table) during each hand, which helps keep the game friendly. The ante is the small amount of money or chips—yours might be a dime, for example—that

each player throws into the pot before every hand. With an ante, each hand is guaranteed to have at least a small payout, even if no one bets after the cards are dealt.

3. If you're playing with chips rather than actual money, decide how much each color is worth with the other players. If you have a standard set with blue, red, and white chips, blues are typically worth the most, then reds, then whites. You might assign the blue chips a worth of one dollar, while the reds would be worth fifty cents, and the whites a dime.

4. If you're playing for money but using chips, buy them now—say, thirty of the cheapest chips, fifteen of the mid-priced ones, and five of the priciest. You can always buy more chips mid-game if you want.

5. Put your ante into the pot.

6. Once all the players have put in the ante, five cards have been dealt to everyone, and the remainder of the deck has been put down in the middle of the table, look at your hand. If you're not sure what you've got, here are the hands from best to worst:

royal flush	ten, jack, queen, king, and ace, all of the same suit
straight flush	five cards in order of the same suit
four of a kind	four cards of the same denomination but of different suits
full house	three of a kind and a pair
flush	five cards of the same suit but not in order
straight	five cards in order but of different suits
three of a kind	three cards of the same denomination but of different suits
two pairs	two sets of two cards of the same denomination but of different suits
one pair	two cards of the same denomination but of different suits
highest card	if no one has anything better, the highest card in the remaining players' hands wins the pot

7. Decide if you want to bet or not based on the cards you have and whether you think you'd be able to come up with a winning hand once you got the

chance to trade in up to three new cards (if this sounds confusing, see step 11).

8. Look innocent. No matter what cards you're holding, good or bad, don't let on or it could affect the way others bet—and lose you money.

9. Wait for your turn to bet (the person to the left of the dealer goes first). If no one's bet already and you're not sure if you want to either, say you'd like to check, which means you want to see what the other players do before you do anything. If you already know you want to put money down, go ahead and open the betting with as small or big a bet as you please (as long as it's within the betting limit) by saying, for example, "I'll open with a dollar." Or, if think your hand is hopeless, say you want to fold, put your cards facedown on the table (not showing them to other players), and watch the rest of the hand play out without you. Yes, you'll lose whatever you've already bet, but it's better than losing even more. If someone's already opened the betting before your turn and you don't want to fold, you have to either see or raise her bet. Seeing a bet just means you're matching the same amount that's already been wagered, while raising it means that you're, uh, raising it. So let's say another player

opened the betting with a dollar. You could say, "I'll see your dollar" and put a dollar in yourself, or you could say, "I'll see your dollar and raise you a dollar" and throw in two bucks.

10. If you've already bet and a player after you raises your bet, play will come back around to you, so start thinking about what to do next. When it's your turn again, you'll have to either match any raises that have been made since your last bet or fold. The game continues like this until no one wants to bet any more, you reach your betting limit, or everyone except one person folds (in which case that player wins). If you're the only one who hasn't folded, don't show your hand—that way, if you were bluffing, the other players won't know, and the less they learn about your betting style, the better.

11. Assuming you didn't fold already, as soon as the betting's over and it's your turn again, you can trade in up to three cards for new ones from the deck in the middle of the table. (The dealer puts discards aside facedown in a separate pile until the next hand, when they'll be shuffled back in the deck.) Don't let anyone see the cards you're getting rid of or the new cards you get. By the way, if you

already have a royal flush, don't worry, you don't have to trade in any cards if you don't want to.

12. If no one's placed a bet on the next round by the time it's your turn, you can check, open the betting, or fold. If the betting's already started, assuming you don't want to fold, you have to either match or raise whatever the person before you bet. Again, the game keeps going like this until no one's up for betting any more money, you reach your betting limit, or everyone except one person folds (in which case that person wins).

13. Turn your cards over and see who has the highest hand. If it's you, take the pot. Congratulations! If there's a tie, the player with the highest card in her hand (meaning full house, pair, or whatever) wins.

14. At the end of the night, if you're using chips in place of money, trade in any you have left for cash.

HOW TO REMOVE CANDLE WAX
FROM A TABLECLOTH

 -

So you borrowed your great-aunt's linen tablecloth only to get drunk at your own dinner party and ignore the candle wax dripping all over it by the end of the evening. No need to fess up when you can clean up instead:

1. Let the wax dry out and harden by putting the cloth in the freezer overnight.

2. Scrape off the surface wax with a dull table knife.

3. Place paper towels on both sides of the stain and press a warm iron over the top one for a couple of seconds to start absorbing the wax.

4. Move the paper towels so there's a fresh area on both sides of the stain and iron again. Keep moving them and ironing until no traces of the wax appear on the towels.

5. Place the stain facedown on a clean paper towel and treat it from behind with a pre-wash stain remover.

6. Blot with a paper towel.

7. Let dry, then wash as usual.

HOW TO RESCUE AN EARRING THAT'S FALLEN DOWN THE DRAIN

- -

While washing your face before bed, one of your earrings inexplicably—though not inextricably!—comes loose and falls down the drain. Here's how to retrieve it:

1. Turn off the faucet immediately.

2. Look under the sink for a U-, S-, or P-shaped piece of pipe, also known as the sink trap.

3. Put a bucket under the sink trap.

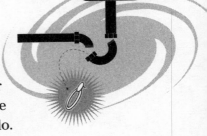

4. See if there's a removable plug (called the cleanout plug) at the bottom of your sink trap. Not all sinks have cleanout plugs, but many do.

5. If there is a cleanout plug, use a wrench or groove-joint pliers to take it off, letting water and any

debris fall in the bucket. If the earring doesn't fall out on its own, unbend a wire hanger so you can probe around in the sink trap with it. Don't be surprised if you run into hair and gunk in the trap, since that's what it's designed for, but hopefully you'll find the earring as well. If you do find it, use your wrench or pliers to put the cleanout plug back on, wash off your earring (be careful not to drop it!), and congratulate yourself.

6. If that doesn't work, or there's no cleanout plug in the first place, you'll have to remove the entire sink trap. Put masking or duct tape around the teeth of your wrench or pliers so they don't wreck your pipe fittings' chrome finish, then loosen one of the slip nuts (those ring-looking things connecting the trap to the rest of the pipe). Support the pipe with one hand while you loosen the other slip nut, then remove the trap. Turn the trap upside down over the bucket, letting it catch any water and debris. The earring should fall out at the same time. If it doesn't, push an unbent wire hanger in and out of the trap to clear any hair and soap scum clogs that might be ensnaring your earring. Once the earring appears, replace the trap and tighten the slip nuts.

HOW TO MAKE AN OMELET

 -

So you're hosting friends for the weekend and want to swiftly whip up a swell Sunday brunch. Your best bet? Omelets! Mix up some mimosas and, sister, you're set. Here's all you need to get cracking:

1. Get all your ingredients together before you start cooking. To make an omelet for one person, you'll need two large eggs, a quarter-teaspoon of salt, a quarter-teaspoon of black pepper, a half-tablespoon of butter, and a tablespoon of fresh herbs (such as basil, tarragon, or cilantro) if you want to be fancy. If you want to make omelets for more than one person, just increase the ingredients accordingly, but keep in mind that you can only cook one serving at a time.

2. Omelets are quite lovely (and easiest) plain, but if you want to add a filling, prepare it now. Try a third of a cup of grated cheese or finely diced ham per omelet, for example. Have a hankering for onion or

veggies? No problem—just chop a third of a cup per omelet and sauté in a teaspoon of butter in a separate nonstick pan first. If you want several filling ingredients, go for it—just keep in mind that you should have about a third of a cup total per omelet.

3. Using a whisk or fork, mix eggs just enough to combine the yolks and whites, then season with salt and pepper (plus herbs, if you're using them). For a fluffier omelet, add a couple of tablespoons of water to the eggs and beat till frothy.

4. Gather everything you'll need on the counter near the stove: a spatula, a plate, a wooden spoon, the butter, the egg mixture, and any filling ingredients. If you're making more than one omelet, divide out a serving of the egg mixture and the filling ingredients before you start cooking—things will go way too fast once the omelet is underway. Measure a third of a cup of egg mixture (which is equal to two eggs) and a third of a cup of filling ingredients per serving.

5. Get a small (about eight inches across) nonstick skillet or omelet pan going over medium heat. If you have a gas stove, give the pan thirty seconds to heat up; with an electric stove, you'll need about three minutes.

6. Add the half-tablespoon of butter to the hot skillet and quickly tilt it back and forth so the butter coats the pan's entire surface, including the sides.

7. Immediately pour the eggs into the hot skillet with one hand and shake the pan back and forth on the burner with the other.

8. As soon as you're finished pouring, grab your wooden spoon and whisk the eggs lightly in the pan for about a minute to incorporate the raw egg with the cooked parts.

9. Resume shaking the skillet back and forth on the burner until the eggs begin to set and you can feel the omelet sliding freely over the pan's surface, which should take about thirty seconds more.

10. If you're adding any filling, spoon it in a line down the middle of the omelet, perpendicular to the pan handle.

11. When the omelet is set but still moist on the surface, turn up the heat to medium-high for ten to fifteen seconds to brown the bottom. Then take the skillet off the burner.

12. Tilt the skillet away from you and use a heatproof rubber spatula to quickly lift and fold the closest third of the omelet over the rest of it.

13. Slide the omelet halfway onto a plate by tilting the pan toward it. Then quickly flip the pan over so the omelet folds over itself again.

14. Throw a sprig of parsley on the side, if you're partial to such things, and serve immediately.

Before you start swimming with pool sharks, you have to get your feet wet. But don't fret—sinking a shot on cue just takes a little practice. Here, the basics on setting up a shot and hitting a ball:

1. Pick up a cue stick and stand facing the pool table with your feet spread about shoulder-width apart. If you're right-handed, lean toward the table by moving your left foot forward and slightly bending your left knee while keeping your right leg straight. If you're left-handed, do the opposite—right foot forward, right knee bent, left leg straight. Your weight should be evenly distributed.

2. Using the hand you write with, grip the thick part of the stick (firmly but not tightly) about ten to twelve inches from the end.

3. Bend over the table and place your other hand palm down on the surface of the table, with fingers

spread, about six to eight inches away from the white cue ball.

4. Using the hand that's touching the table, make a bridge to support the narrow end of the stick by raising your knuckles slightly, but keeping your fingertips and the heel of your hand on the table. Raise your thumb off the table, then press the base of your thumb against the side of your hand, bending the tip of your thumb back slightly. You should be able to slide the stick smoothly back and forth between your thumb and the side of your hand.

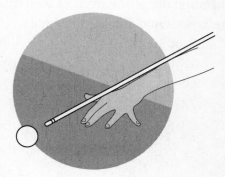

5. Make sure there's no one behind you, then loosen up with a few practice strokes of the stick. Pull your elbow back so the top of your arm is parallel to the table and your forearm hangs straight down.

Keeping the stick as level as possible and your wrist relaxed, move your forearm back and forth. The top of your arm should remain parallel to the table and the rest of your body should stay as still as possible. Swing your forearm like a pendulum, moving from your elbow, not your shoulder.

6. Decide which target ball you want to hit with the cue ball. Your goal is to use the cue ball to hit the target ball and make that target ball (but not the cue ball) drop into a pocket. In order to know where to aim, imagine there's a line stretching from the pocket through the target ball. The spot where the line would come out at the front of the target ball is where you should aim the cue ball.

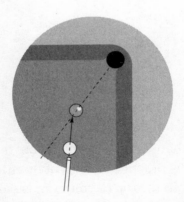

7. Make your shot by hitting the cue ball solidly with a smooth, level stroke. Your forearm should be at a ninety-degree angle to the table as the tip of the stick hits the cue ball.

8. Follow through on your shot by staying down in position and extending your arm so the tip of your stick moves a few inches past where the cue ball was located. At the same time, the target ball should be dropping into the pocket.

HOW TO RESCUE AN OVERBAKED CAKE

69

Let them eat cake! Okay, so you didn't hear the timer go off and your chocolate layers got a little charbroiled. Not to worry—a few quick tricks and you can still have your cake and eat it too:

1. Take the cake out of the oven immediately.

2. Fill your sink with cold water until it comes about halfway up the sides of the cake pan(s), then throw in a tray of ice cubes.

3. Leave the cake pan(s) in the sink for about five minutes to cool the cake as quickly as possible.

4. Remove the pan(s) from the sink and let the cake cool completely.

5. Boil a half-cup of sugar and a quarter-cup of water in a saucepan for about three minutes over high heat until the sugar dissolves.

6. Cool the mixture to room temperature. If you want to add a little extra zip, stir in a tablespoon of rum, brandy, amaretto, Frangelico, Kahlua, or Grand Marnier.

7. If it's a layer cake, put the first layer upside-down on the serving plate and put the other layer aside.

8. Use a sharp knife to lightly score the surface of the cake about every half-inch in both directions.

9. Very slowly drizzle about a quarter of the sugar syrup over the cake, being careful not to let it drip over the sides any more than you can avoid. Once that's sunk in, drizzle on another quarter. If it's a layer cake, put the rest of the syrup aside. Otherwise, drizzle the rest on now.

10. Add two teaspoons of milk to your frosting so it's a little thinner than usual. This will help the cake taste moister and make it easier to spread on the scored surface.

11. Ice the cake from the middle outward—don't use a back-and-forth spreading motion or you'll get crumbs in your frosting. If it's a layer cake, ice

the first layer, then add the second, score it, and give it the syrup treatment before frosting it.

12. Cut the cake into pieces. If it's a nine-by-thirteen-inch cake, trim off the sides before serving.

13. If you have any ice cream or whipped cream on hand, serve some with the cake for an even more moist dessert.

It's the morning after a few too many, and you're hibernating in bed, swearing off liquor for life. Unfortunately, time is the only *true* cure for a nasty hangover, but there are several things you can do to soothe the pain of a pounding head, queasy stomach, and the other miseries of overindulging:

1. Keep drinking before you head to bed, but make sure your beverage of choice changes to water— and lots of it. Alcohol is a diuretic, so a nightcap of H_2O will help minimize dehydration and make your hangover less severe the next morning.

2. Take aspirin or Advil for your headache, but avoid painkillers containing acetaminophen (such as Tylenol and Anacin). Although it's true that aspirin or Advil can exacerbate an upset stomach, they're preferable to taking anything with acetaminophen, which has been shown in several studies to cause liver damage in people who've been drinking heavily.

3. When you wake up, chug Gatorade and/or more water. Coffee might help fight a headache, but be aware that java, like all caffeinated drinks, is a diuretic and will aggravate dehydration.

4. To combat the nausea and jitters caused by the low blood sugar from last night's alcohol intake, consume foods high in carbohydrates, such as cereal, crackers, and bread or toast, and drink cranberry juice or other fruit juices high in sugar (just avoid citrus juices on an upset stomach). A little low-fat protein—a scrambled egg, say, or a turkey sandwich—will help you regain energy. Stay away from burgers and fries and other high-fat, high-sodium foods, however; the fat may make you nauseous, and the sodium will just make you more dehydrated.

HOW MUCH TO TIP

Feeling tipsy? When you want to leave a little extra something, but have no idea just how little or extra that something should be, keep in mind that the gold standard of gratuities is fifteen percent of the bill. That said, there are a few finer tipping points you should know before you can truly call yourself civilized. Here's a cheat sheet on who gets what:

- **Apartment building doorman:** If he goes above and beyond the call of his regular duties—like, say, he waters a couple of houseplants while you're on a trip or helps you carry a bunch of cases of beer upstairs before a party—give him an extra five or ten dollars. Around the holidays, tip him twenty to a hundred dollars depending on which part of the country you live in, how fancy your building is, and what you can afford. Give more if you have a home business, get lots of deliveries, and/or always receive prompt and courteous assistance. (Standard procedure for tipping around the holidays: go to the bank and get crisp, new bills, stick them in an envelope with a card, and hand them to the recipient in person.)

- **_Apartment building superintendent:_** Around the holidays, tip twenty-five to seventy-five dollars, depending on where you live.

- **_Bartender:_** A good rule of thumb is one dollar per beer or wine, two dollars per mixed drink, but always tip at least twenty percent for courteous service. If a bartender gives you a free drink after a couple of rounds, tip him half of what the drink would've cost you. So, for example, if he offers you a six-dollar gimlet, give him three bucks (hey, you'll still come out ahead).

- **_Bellhop:_** One to two dollars per bag.

- **_Coat checker:_** One dollar per coat or bag.

- **_Coffee or ice cream shop counter person:_** Tipping isn't required, but toss fifty cents or a buck in the tip jar if you're feeling flush and the service is friendly and efficient (especially if you've asked for three sherbet samples or a couple of teapot refills).

- **_Concierge:_** If she gets you reservations at a hot restaurant or tickets to a sold-out show, tip her twenty bucks.

- ***Dog walker:*** At the holidays, tip the cost of one day's work.

- ***Hairdresser:*** Fifteen to twenty percent to the stylist; three to five dollars to the shampooer. And forget anything you may have heard about not tipping a salon owner who doubles as a stylist—that's no longer not done. Around the holidays, tip your stylist the price of a regular session or give a non-cash gift.

- ***Handyman:*** Tipping's not required, but if he fixes your air conditioner on the double on the hottest day of the year, give him an extra five to ten dollars. Around the holidays, give him fifteen to twenty-five dollars—more if he's especially handy to you throughout the year.

- ***Hotel maid:*** One to two dollars for each night of your stay, left on the pillow or dresser (with a note saying "Thank you!" so the maid knows it's for her) when you leave the room each morning.

- ***Mail carrier:*** The postal service prohibits mail carriers from accepting cash gifts, but a holiday tip in the form of something small with a value of under twenty bucks, such as candy or baked goods, is allowed.

- *Maitre d':* Not required, but occasionally slipping the maitre d' at your favorite restaurant ten or twenty bucks at the end of the night for giving you a good table and ensuring great service should keep the good times coming.

- *Manicurist/pedicurist:* Fifteen to twenty percent.

- *Masseur or masseuse:* Ten dollars per hour, though you should ask at the front desk if gratuities are included, since they often are.

- *Newspaper carrier:* Around the holidays, tip ten to twenty dollars.

- *Personal trainer:* Tip the cost of one session during the holiday season.

- *Pizza delivery guy:* Fifteen percent or at least two dollars. Toss in an extra buck for deliveries in bad weather or over long distances.

- *Restroom attendant at a fancy restaurant or theater:* One dollar.

- *Shoeshiner:* One to two dollars per pair.

- *Skycap:* One to two dollars per bag.

- *Tailor, cobbler, dry cleaner:* You don't have to tip anything, but if it's especially good work or a rush job, tip fifteen percent.

- *Taxi driver:* Fifteen percent or at least one dollar. If you're in a hurry, promise the driver a big tip to get you there pronto and add an extra five dollars to what you'd have normally tipped anyway.

- *Valet parking attendant:* One to two dollars when the car is returned. If you know you'll need to make a speedy exit, give the attendant ten bucks beforehand to keep the car close by.

- *Waiter:* At least fifteen percent for good service; twenty percent in swankier spots or for great service anywhere. Gratuities should always be calculated based on the pre-tax portion of the bill.

- *Wine steward:* If you got substantial advice from a sommelier, thank her by shaking her hand and simultaneously slipping her fifteen percent of the wine tab in cash at the end of dinner. (By the way, when you're tipping the wine steward, tip the waiter on the food portion of the bill only.)

HOW TO READ A PALM

What's the best way to suss out that special someone's secrets—and get to hold his hand at the same time? Read his palms! Okay, this stuff isn't exactly scientific, but, whatever, it's fun. His life is in your hands; all you have to do is know what to look for:

1. Ask your subject which hand he writes with. That's the dominant hand, which reflects his public self and shows what he's made of his life. The other hand, meanwhile, shows the qualities he was born with and reveals the real him. Check both hands throughout your reading to compare and contrast.

2. Look at his hands in relation to his body size. If his hands are small, he's a natural leader and intuitive. If they're large, he's detail-oriented and outdoorsy.

3. Check out the lines on his hands. Lots of lines are the sign of a nervous temperament, while only a few indicate a calm personality.

4. Find the heart line, the highest major line on the hand, which starts under the pinky and extends toward the index finger. This is the line that deals with relationships and emotions. If it goes straight from one edge of his palm to the other, he puts work before love. He's a romantic dreamer if it ends under his index finger; if it goes all the way to the base of that finger, he's a perfectionist with unrealistic standards. If it ends at the web between his index and middle fingers, he's very loving, but tends to express it physically more than verbally. If it ends under his middle finger, he's a player who avoids commitment. A deep heart line means he's generous and fair, while a faint heart line indicates a sentimental personality. If his line is curved, he's passionate and sexual; if it's straight, he's reserved and slow to commit. Does it end in a fork? That means he's understanding, sensible, and popular.

5. Examine the head line, the middle major line, which starts on the thumb side of the palm. If it's straight, he's business-minded, analytical, and materialistic. If it's curved, he's creative and artistic. If the line is deep, he's smart; if it's faint, he's a worrier. If it ends in a fork, he's expressive and successful. And if it ends in three prongs? He's emotional, absent-minded, and extremely intelligent.

6. Look at the life line, the line that starts between the thumb and index finger and arcs toward the wrist. Contrary to popular belief, this line reveals the quality of life, not the length of it. If the line is deep, he's energetic and good at meeting challenges, but if it's faint, he's sensitive and susceptible to sickness. If the arc is wide and ends in the center of the wrist, he's curious, outgoing, and healthy; if it curves back and ends at the base of the thumb, he's introverted and likely to prefer staying in to going out. Do the starting points of the life line and the head line overlap? If so, he's cautious and apt to pay too much attention to what other people think. If the two lines are far apart, however, he's independent, impatient, and spontaneous.

WHAT TO DO IF A BIRD FLIES
IN THE HOUSE

 73

When birds see reflections of trees in your windows, they figure, you know, "Great, more trees!" And sometimes, if you have a window open on a nice day, their bird brains will tell them to just fly right on in. Here's how to make your uninvited guests' stay as short as possible:

1. Shut Fluffy or Fido in another room.

2. Drawing curtains and blinds as you go, close all the room's windows and doors but one. Leave the largest exit to the outside open. If it's dark, turn off any indoor lights and put a light on outside to attract the bird.

3. Close any other interior doors in the house.

4. Put on some Metallica (or the hard rock group of your choice) and crank up the volume. Birds dislike loud noise and, like your parents, will be repelled by your musical taste.

5. Leave the room and let your feathered friend find its way out without having to stress about your hanging around.

6. Check back every fifteen minutes until the bird has flown the coop.

We'd like to thank the following people and organizations for their help in making this book what it is: B.G. Dilworth at Authors and Artists Group; Elizabeth Beier at St. Martin's Press; Bobby, Matt, Katherine, Kevin, and Bob Nix; Jean, George, Jeff and Dave Hurchalla; Kristie Hemenway; Matt Graves; Jennifer Hecht; George Rodgers; Christine Larson; Rich Rojo; Julie Taylor; Jay Brown; Jela Trivunovic; Danya Darrington; Torry Greene; Shelley Pyne-Hanley; Marc Borkan; Gregg Farano; Francis Gasparini; Nancy Kalish; Ivy Garcia; Karl Haller; Stacy Lu; Steven Amsterdam; Rob Buscemi; Dina Maiorana; Dan Woltman; Vince Martinelli; Jill Gibson; David Fannon; Gillian Judge; Chris Harges; Tara Twedt; Lisa Hug; Chris Poole; Stuart Hazleton; Brigid Maher; Margaret McConville; Tom McConville; Marcella Freisen and the ladies of Window Treats in Westfield, New Jersey; Barbara Hofeditz; Brenda Rinard; John Talbot; Wendi Deetz of the Women's Safety Project in San Francisco; Officer Jim Bennett of the Mountain View, California, Police Department; Rene Soltis of the Vision Council of America and checkyearly.com; Dennis Thoele; Jan Wyatt-Lucha, R.D.;

Peter Marks of the American Center for Wine, Food, and the Arts; the Veterans of Foreign Wars; the American Legion; Sam and Matt Morgan; Ali Blum; Lee Ann Moldovanyi; Diane Goodman; Margot Gilman; Steve Johnson; Gregg Schaufeld; Sonya and Jack Howard-Zilka; Hafeez Raji; Michael Merrill; Mike DiBianco; Jane Mount; Megan Brenn-White; the guys at Café Que Tal; and the fine people who manufacture Hershey's Kisses, the snack that makes writing well into the night more fun.